MEASUREMENTS
FOR EFFECTIVE
DECISION MAKING

MEASUREMENTS
FOR EFFECTIVE
DECISION MAKING

A GUIDE FOR
MANUFACTURING
COMPANIES

Mokshagundam L. Srikanth, Ph.D.
Scott A. Robertson

The Spectrum Publishing Company
Guilford, Connecticut

To order additional copies of this text or related texts, please contact:

The Spectrum Publishing Company, Inc.
200 Concept Park
741 Boston Post Road
Guilford, CT 06437
(203)453-2233

For more information on the practical application of the concepts and principles contained in this text, please contact:

The Spectrum Management Group, Inc.
200 Concept Park
741 Boston Post Road
Guilford, CT 06437
(203)453-2233

Library of Congress Cataloging-in-Publication Data

Srikanth, Mokshagundam L., 1952-
      Measurements for effective decision making : a guide for
manufacturing companies / Mokshagundam L. Srikanth, Scott A.
Robertson.
            p.   cm.
      Includes bibliographical references.
      ISBN 0-943953-04-9
      1. Manufactures — Management. 2. Manufactures — Cost control.
3. Decision making. 4. Cost accounting. I. Robertson, Scott A.,
1959-   . II. Title.
HD9720.5.S68 1995
670'.68'4—dc20   95-9547
                                                                        CIP

Manufactured in the United States of America

*To my wife Geri-Lee for her love,
support and understanding.
- M.L.S.*

*To Janine, Erin and Jake for your constant
love, patience and support.
- S.A.R.*

Contents

Acknowledgments

The measurement approach presented in this book was forged into a viable product from some raw concepts in many client implementations over the past several years. Our foremost and deepest gratitude goes to our clients for the faith, courage and persistence they showed in developing and implementing the new measurement system.

The "In-Sync" system presented in this book is simple; it is powerful and it works. Our colleagues at Spectrum deserve much of the credit for the development and refinement of the "In-Sync" system. We are the voice for the collective learning and experience of The Spectrum Management Group. We are responsible for the organization and presentation of the material; lack of clarity and errors are entirely our responsibility.

Jon Zonderman converted our discussions and rough drafts into a readable manuscript. Albert Cubelli helped make sure that the rules of the English language were not seriously infringed. To both our sincere thanks. Graham Side and Khiem Dang deserve special recognition for the admirable job they did in managing the "book project."

Introduction

A great deal has been written and published in recent years concerning the apparent demise of the standard cost system. The idea that this accounting approach is ill-suited for today's competitive environment has become mainstream. Yet, to paraphrase Mark Twain, "rumors of its death are greatly exaggerated." Although it is clear that this system is outdated, there is confusion concerning alternatives. There has been seemingly endless debate concerning Activity-Based Costing (ABC) as well as other approaches for allocating costs to products. Yet the issue remains unresolved. What remains for those expected to persevere through this search is many unanswered questions and an empty feeling that daily decision making is founded on faulty assumptions.

This book is an attempt to fill at least some of this void. It is not intended as an alternative to the standard cost accounting system, but rather as an alternative decision making system to the one spawned by this accounting approach. In tracing the history of the standard cost approach to allocating cost, one recognizes a clear divergence from the system as an accounting convention to the system as a management tool for decision making. The leap to performance measures based on direct labor hours was a short one. This book attempts to provide a structured answer to the question: *If the standard cost-based measures are discredited, then what are the appropriate performance measures for today's competitive marketplace?*

Clearly, measurement systems for decision making and for evaluating performance are a powerful tool management wields in the day-to-day battle of manufacturing. The ability to determine agenda, to set priorities and to focus activities are all contained within this tool. Unfortunately, this power often goes unrecognized. Organizations develop a hodge-podge approach to their measurement system with its foundation still laid in the faulty logic of the standard cost system. Interestingly, many organizations in the throes of the cost accounting debate don't even recognize that most of their internal metrics are based on the same system their financial people are actively questioning.

Our experience in implementing synchronous management techniques in a variety of environments has provided the foundation for this book. All too often managers have been laboring under systems that are poorly aligned with market realities. This misalignment is found not only in measurement and decision making systems but in operating methods and organizational mindset as well. The approach we have embraced involves making each of these elements self-consistent with each other as well as the external marketplace. The necessity for developing this set of self-consistent measures is obvious. Further, we believe that the philosophy of synchronous management provides the best schematic for an approach appropriate for today's environment.

The implementation approach delineated is, by necessity, generic. The successful development and application of an alternative measures set is always a tricky undertaking requiring explicit support from both senior management and the financial community. We hope that this book will be useful in helping the reader in this necessary endeavor. We welcome any input, comments or questions.

CHAPTER 1

OLD MEASURES DON'T SERVE NEW MARKET REALITIES

In the early part of the century, football was a simple game. It consisted of the quarterback handing the ball to a running back, who ran straight ahead. The offensive line's job was to move the defensive line back. The defensive team's job was to fight off the blocking and tackle the man with the ball.

Teams trained to build strength. They practiced to enhance strength. They were judged on strength. And, in the end, strength often prevailed. The culture, or mindset, of the professional football industry could be summarized as "Football is a game of strength." The key measure consistent with this mindset was individual player strength.

But over the years, football has changed dramatically. The range of offensive plays has steadily grown. First, there was the development of a passing game, utilizing increasingly speedy wide receivers. Then came the advent of quicker running backs who could run wide as well as through the line. Then there were passes to running backs coming out from behind the line of scrimmage. Then there was the advent of the strong, big tight end who was also an excellent receiver. The game was becoming more complex, and success depended on players with attributes other than mere strength. Speed, quickness and game intelligence were also important and could be more useful than strength alone.

While all of this was happening, some teams were quicker to see the trends than others. The teams that caught on signed players with an increasingly wide range of skills. They trained for speed, quickness, agility, and flexibility, as well as strength. They trained the defense to handle offenses that had speed, quickness, agility, and flexibility.

The teams that were not so quick to catch on to the changing trends of the game continued to sign big, strong players. They continued to train for strength, practice for strength, and measure only strength.

Guess which teams will play in next year's Super Bowl?

The manufacturing industry has gone through an evolution similar to the one described above. Through much of this century, demand exceeded capacity, and the market was dictated by producers, i.e. a sellers' market. Sales, and hence company growth, were practically assured. The focus of manufacturing activities was on controlling costs; with sales assured, cost control would ensure profits. The standard cost accounting system made direct labor efficiency the critical focal point for controlling production costs. Naturally, manufacturing in this period evolved the mindset:

"Manufacturing is an efficiency machine."

It is commonly recognized by today's manufacturing professionals that the traditional American approach to managing production operations must be fundamentally altered if the U.S. is to regain a competitive edge in world markets. While significant effort has gone into this transformation in the years since the early 1980s, much more still needs to be done.

By the middle of the 20th century's final decade, many companies have at least begun to defeat what we call "the mass production mentality" by the way they organize manufacturing operations. The mass production mentality, which follows the lead of Henry Ford, creates facilities geared to producing the highest volume of standardized products at the lowest possible cost. Management, acting within this mentality, is focused on maximizing unit volume and minimizing unit cost.

The mass production approach worked extremely well in the environment where demand exceeded capacity, where demand was constantly rising, and the producer could set a price that included a profit above production costs. This sellers' market characterized the American marketplace preceding, and especially immediately following, the second World War. The formula below captures the relative ease with which profits could be assured. It worked in a period of cheap money, which could be easily borrowed to diversify and add plants and product lines.

Price	=	Cost	+	Profit
(set by producer)		(to manufacture)		(desired by producer)

Today, however, worldwide capacity exceeds demand and the global market has become much more focused on quality, product diversity, and customer service than simply on low cost. Capital is expensive. Prices are dictated by the market and not by the producer. The formula below captures the fact that the "certainty" of profits has been removed as price competition has become fierce.

Price	=	Cost	+	Profit
(set by market)		(to manufacture)		(if any)

The producer's profit, and not the price, becomes the variable. The new mass production is as ill-suited to meeting these challenges as a 1930s-style football team's defensive unit would be at meeting the challenges posed by today's flexible offense.

Moving in lock step with the mass production approach is the "scientific school" of management created primarily by Frederick Taylor. The scientific system of production management breaks down operational tasks into their simplest elements. These elements can then either be automated or "de-skilled" to the point where essentially any person can be easily trained to perform the simple, repetitive tasks involved. The scientific method was also the foundation for paying workers on a piecework basis.

While in many cases this leads to higher unit volumes, it also results in narrow functional specialization and a tendency to achieve local optimization regardless of the effects on any other operations. In effect, it creates the attitude — "my piece rate goes up, and I make more money; who cares what happens to you?" — and results in the de-coupling of activities that should naturally be integrated. People lose sight of "why" they are doing things and do not understand how their task impacts the flow of products and services to the customer. It also creates a situation where man and machine are seen by management as interchangeable, and decisions regarding automation are made on a strict volume/cost basis. The entire mindset of scientific management contributes to severe morale problems.

Running production operations based on the scientific method worked well in a sellers' market, when production volume really was the key to success. In the buyers' market of today, however, with its high premium on quality, product diversity and customer service, tasks need to be recombined and the work force must be increasingly "re-skilled." Human resources must be seen as appreciating rather than depreciating assets and need to be developed more highly than ever before.

The third piece of the traditional manufacturing triad, along with the mass production mentality and the scientific method, is the standard cost accounting system. Since the time of Ford and Taylor, day-to-day activities at all levels of the manufacturing organization have been governed by the standard cost accounting system and its single-minded focus on the reduction of unit costs through the reduction of direct labor content.

The result is a management mindset in which the primary focus, at all levels of the organization, is on "productivity" and efficiency. In this environment, productivity is defined as every worker working all of the time and at least as fast as the engineered standard. The only productive activity is producing parts or "cutting chips." Successful companies of today realize that other appropriate and necessary work includes maintenance, training, etc., and should be included in our concept of productive utilization of resources.

There are two major problems with the traditional approach. First, the total and obsessive focus on production cost is not appropriate in the buyers' market. It is also not the best system in a sellers' market, although it can be, at times, adequate. Second, the detailed methods and techniques that have arisen from the focus on efficiency are invalid in today's complex, dynamic, and interdependent manufacturing environment.

These methods and techniques may actually contribute to increased product cost. Efforts to optimize each operation to 100 percent local efficiency ultimately creates a completely unbalanced manufacturing operation and costs dearly in terms of inventory and defects. (For a detailed discussion of this point see References 1, 2, 3.)

The new production system is captured by the mindset:

"Manufacturing is a sales driver."

It represents the fact that activities in manufacturing should have as their primary focus the delivery of goods and services that satisfy customers. This focus can be used as a competitive advantage. Generating a steady stream of revenues through superior customer satisfaction should be the number one priority for all manufacturing and operations personnel. This is not to say that costs or expenses are not an issue. It simply asserts that customer satisfaction is a priority. The challenge is to find a way of doing this profitably.

In the vocabulary of synchronous management, there is an important distinction made between the words "activation" and "utilization." Activation is defined as simply the employment of a resource to process materials. In contrast, utilization means the employment of a resource to process materials in order to meet scheduled demand. Under the old way of thinking there is no distinction; activation is the same as utilization. In a sellers' market, this was, for all intents and purposes, true. Since there was always demand, to activate was in effect to utilize. Of course, as summarized by the synchronous principles outlined in chapter 2 and amply demonstrated by the accomplishments of just-in-time implementations, even in a sellers' market, plain activation results in waste. Focusing on utilization rather than activation makes for better profits in all market conditions.

It should not come as a surprise that the standard cost accounting system evolved in the direction of tracking and controlling direct labor activity. Standards were developed to three and four decimal accuracy, and performance was tracked to these standards. Every operator had to account for every minute he was not working on producing product. It was expected that this lost time would be tracked and categorized, and the root cause would be eliminated. Most shop data collection systems today are designed precisely for this purpose. Note that implicit in this is the assumption that labor (and material) variances were always the root cause issues!

COST ACCOUNTING LOSES RELEVANCE

The logic that if an operator is not producing product then he is simply costing money seems obvious. But that is only because of the cost accounting system that grew up around mass production and the scientific method. And, as is becoming increasingly obvious, the conventions of standard cost accounting have no bearing on the reality in which companies find themselves in today's market environment.

Standard cost accounting was originally a financial tool developed to measure unit costs in a mass production environment. And as such it was a success. While industrial and mechanical engineers were developing standards for the discreet activities within production processes, accountants worked on a parallel track to create standard costs for the use of direct labor and materials within those tasks.

Indirect costs were allocated evenly across product units. This was fine for a business that produced a narrow range of products, had indirect costs that were a fraction of direct costs and material, and was efficiently mass producing products that were gobbled up by growing market demand.

After World War II, standard cost accounting was projected from a purely accounting methodology into a management approach. This was a simple outgrowth of the notion that the cost system and its calculations provided a bridge between local production activities and corporate financial performance. If the "numbers" provided by the standard cost system could link local work center and department activities to company profits, then they could be used to guide and evaluate operating supervisors and managers. As such, the standard cost accounting methodology spawned related performance measures based upon that assumption.

"Management by the numbers" became the rage, and the numbers used for this purpose (such as return on controllable assets, unit costs, shop costs, etc.) all were derived through the application of the standard cost system. It was a small step to then use these numbers as the measure of managerial performance. And once return on assets, unit cost, shop cost, etc. became the operative performance measures, the entire management hierarchy began to make each and every decision through the lens of the standard cost system. We will use the term standard cost system in this book to include the measures (such as unit cost, earned hours, labor efficiency, unit margin, etc.) that the standard accounting system engenders.

For two generations, the standard cost system was used by hundreds of thousands of manufacturing managers as they sought the correct answer to their capital investment decisions, personnel utilization decisions, and even product development decisions. And, for two generations, the calculations usually told them that an investment in labor-saving technologies was a good one, that adding indirect labor didn't matter because it would be amortized over each unit, and that developing more products would be a way to utilize excess capacity.

But during this management generation (running from approximately 1950-1990), the rules of the manufacturing game changed drastically. During those 40 years, the game changed to such an extent that the standard cost system became obsolete as a tool for making these various kinds of decisions.

From the end of the second World War until the present, the typical manufacturing company has added far more indirect labor employees than direct labor workers. It has added layers of personnel to handle management information, to design product and support the production process, and to provide the marketing, sales and services customers are demanding more frequently.

Fortunately, companies are increasingly breaking down the mass production mindset and recognizing that activities must be re-integrated and re-skilled. And few companies continue to pay workers on a piecework basis. But too often they continue to measure the "effectiveness" of activities using the standard cost system. The question for managers is: "If we don't pay piecework wages, then why do we measure people and activities on a piecework basis?"

What has happened over the last 40 years of American manufacturing is that many companies have assumed that the standard cost-based measures provide a solid bridge from the macro goal of a manufacturing business — to make money — to the micro activities of the factory floor.

But the mass production mindset, the scientific method and, most egregiously, the standard cost system, too often lead managers to make decisions as if the goal were to maintain productivity as measured by direct labor efficiency. Today, the problems of the standard cost system as a decision making tool are clearly recognized by the accounting profession. (For a full history of cost accounting and some of its shortcomings, refer to the book *Relevance Lost: The Rise And Fall Of Management Accounting* by Robert Kaplan and Thomas Johnson.[4])

A "BALANCED AND STRUCTURED SET" OF MANUFACTURING MEASURES

It is our goal in this book to create a set of measures to be used by manufacturing companies. We call the set of measures **In-Sync.** This structured set is an outgrowth of the work of many people who, since the early 1990s, have been calling for a more balanced approach to performance measures. Some, most notably the Harvard Business School Professor Robert Kaplan, call such an approach "The Balanced Scorecard."[5]

We want to instill throughout the organization — from the board room to the factory floor — the idea of the balanced scorecard performance measurement system. This is the objective of our In-Sync set of measures. The fact is that in today's market-place, customers are more demanding, and there is strong competition for many, if not most, goods and services. Because of this, performance must be measured by how well customers are "satisfied" in their desire for products and services. The focus of the measures should be to determine how well the company's goods and services meet customer needs and desires for quality, service, product attributes, and a host of other criteria.

In today's competitive markets the purely internal focus of the standard cost system is inappropriate. Customers must be satisfied if they are to continue buying a particular company's products and services. This revenue stream is the prerequisite to generating profits. Manufacturing businesses must manage the balance between maintaining high levels of customer service and generating decent profits. The measurement system must reflect both the external (or customer) side and the internal (or cost) side of the business. Only with this information can a balance be established and maintained.

The reality of competitive markets has forced companies to begin measuring items such as customer satisfaction and quality. As shown in Figure 1-1, the result is a patchwork of measures and indicators that have been developed over the years in an ad hoc manner. Traditional measures tie manufacturing activities to business profits through the standard cost system, which is driven by labor reporting. The ad hoc measures (shown on the right of the figure) grew as the need for a more comprehensive set of indicators became clear. However, there is no clear relationship between the ad hoc measures and business profits.

A large variety of indicators do exist, but they are not always consistent and do not measure different functions and levels the same way. The measures and indicators are well-intentioned, but their impact on actual decision making is diminished by two factors. One, some of these "new" indicators are also products of the standard cost system. They simply massage the old set of numbers into a new set. Two, those numbers that do not fall into this category, and therefore may have new and useful information, lose significance and impact since they are outside the mainstream accounting and budgeting system.

The In-Sync set of measures attempts to replace the standard cost system as the crucial bridge between operational activities and the financial performance of the company (see Figure 1-2). It provides for a set of measures that include customer satisfaction, competitive performance, and cost performance. In-Sync is designed to be consistent and provide for a balance between external and internal aspects of a company's performance. It is designed to answer the two questions:

- Are the company's customers satisfied?
- Is the company making money?

Figure 1-1

Lack of linkage between ad hoc measures and operating performance/business profits.

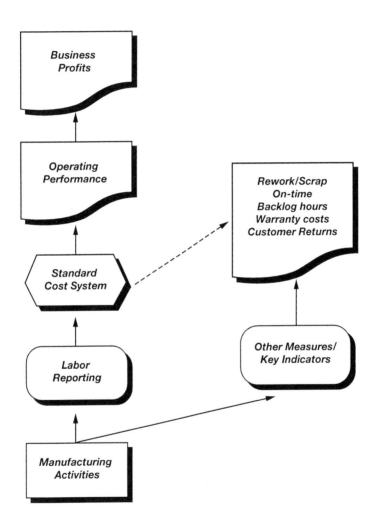

Figure 1-2

In-Sync® replaces the host of traditional indicators with a consistent, structured and balanced set of measures which ties manufacturing activities directly to business profits.

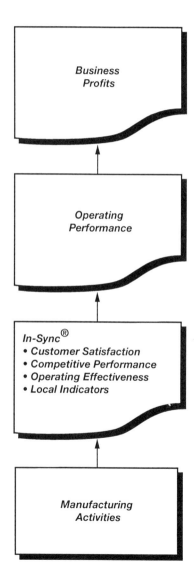

Finally, In-Sync includes a process and a set of indicators that focus the organization toward specific improvements that are crucial to improving the performance of the entire business. It can provide specific local guidance without losing overall business relevance. The key objectives of the In-Sync set are to:

- enable all employees to align daily actions with overall company goals.
- support decisions that serve to add value.
- provide a balance between the internal and external focus of all employees.

In-Sync is a natural outgrowth of our earlier synchronous manufacturing and later synchronous management methodologies. In order to create the kind of behavioral changes necessary to keep employees (from management to shop floor workers) aligned with synchronous concepts, it is necessary to change the measures that govern the way people and their actions are viewed and appraised. Every manufacturer should ask himself, "If I'm not going to manage my manufacturing operation the old way, then how can I continue to measure people and activities in the old way?"

Chapter 2 of this book provides a brief introduction to the concepts of synchronous management. For those who have read our books on synchronous manufacturing, much of this material will be familiar. We urge those unfamiliar with the synchronous concepts in this book to seek other volumes on this subject (see References 1, 2, 3).

Chapters 3-7 describe the structured set of measures. These measures are broken up into four groups: 1) Customer focus measures, 2) Competitive measures, 3) Operational (asset management) measures, and 4) Internal micro measures (local indicators).

Chapters 8 and 9 walk the reader through exercises on how to use the new, structured set of measures when making decisions on capital expenditures, as well as product cost and product mix decisions.

Finally, chapter 10 examines some of the organizational and logistical issues involved in the transition from the old set of measures to the new structured set.   This extensive change in a business' approach to management will create culture shock. We have not tried to write a chapter about change management; many others have done that far better than we could in one chapter.

CHAPTER 2

SYNCHRONOUS MANAGEMENT AN INTRODUCTION

The transition from the traditional American system of mass production to one that is consistent with today's challenges and opportunities requires an entirely new management approach. There have been many previous attempts to change one or more of the major components of management effort, such as total quality management (TQM) and just-in-time (JIT). While these have often led to some level of improvement, many have fallen short of expectations. Some have tended to be technical in nature, with the behavioral components (i.e. the need for people to change behavior) as afterthoughts. Others have been behavioral in nature, often losing sight of the business reason why the behavior change is so necessary.

Synchronous management is defined as: "an all-encompassing management philosophy which includes a consistent set of principles, procedures and techniques, and which strives to ensure that every action is focused on, and measured in terms of, the common global goal of the organization." That goal is, of course, to make money now and in the future, by creating and delivering products and services that meet customer needs and desires. This approach can be used as an umbrella under which a company can place more process-oriented tools and techniques to enhance business operations.

The balance of this chapter will be devoted to providing an overview of the concepts and techniques of synchronous

19

management.   It is not intended to be comprehensive but rather to provide the reader with some of the fundamentals. For those who wish to pursue this subject in greater detail, please refer to *Synchronous Manufacturing: Principles for World-Class Excellence* by Umble and Srikanth.[1]

The synchronous management approach differs from the traditional approach by focusing on change at three levels: 1) the mindset of the organization, 2) the measures that drive the organization, and 3) the methods of work employed within the organization.

> **Mindset** is defined as the collective way of thinking that organizes the business' approach and determines what is important and what issues are given priority.

> **Measures** are the metrics that serve as quantitative indicators of how effectively a business functions. They serve the dual purpose of guiding decision making and evaluating organizational and managerial performance.

> **Methods** are the techniques employed in the execution of day-to-day activities of people and equipment in the planning, production and delivery of goods and services to the customer.

SYNCHRONOUS, OR LEAN, PRODUCTION OPERATION

Over the past few years, based on extensive studies done by a number of groups such as the MIT Commission on Industrial Productivity,[6] a clear picture of what the new organization will look like has emerged. The new mode of operation has been described with various terms including agile manufacturing, lean production and synchronous manufacturing.

Figure 2-1

Comparison between traditional mass production systems and synchronous systems with respect to several competitive elements.

Competitive Element	Traditional or High-Inventory Operation	Synchronous or Lean Production Operation
Service Responsiveness	Production pipeline clogged, making quick response impossible.	Short manufacturing lead times and "clean" pipelines permit quick deliveries.
Delivery Reliability (On-Time Shipments)	Chaotic shop environment. Constant expediting required to be close to promise on at least some production orders.	Smooth coordinated flow ensures reliable delivery of product.
Price	Quality problems, poor resource utilization, shop chaos, and expediting contribute to high product cost.	Smooth flow leads to improved "utilization" of resources. This and better quality significantly reduce cost.
Quality	Causes are buried in high inventories. Expediting and "firefighting;" leaves no time for fixing the process.	Causes can be quickly and easily identified. Encourages and enables fixing the problem.

The new production mode is a low-inventory mode of operation. The major competitive elements by which manufacturing operations compete are: product features, quality, delivery, responsiveness, service, and price. Figure 2-1 summarizes how a lean production system, or synchronized flow, provides an advantage with respect to each competitive element over more traditional high-inventory production.

While it is increasingly accepted that the traditional mass production manufacturing model is unsuited to today's competitive marketplace, the transition from high-inventory manufacturing to synchronous low-inventory manufacturing continues to be difficult for many companies.

Three factors contribute to the persistence of high-inventory manufacturing. One is that the techniques for managing the complex material flow in real-world production operations in a low-inventory environment were only *rediscovered* recently (remember that Henry Ford's Rouge River facility was a classic low-inventory facility). The second is that the high-inventory mode of production was very successful. This success cannot be overlooked, as it contributes significantly to the current resistance to change. The third, and perhaps most important, factor that helps perpetuate the high-inventory manufacturing environment is the continued use of the traditional standard cost system to make manufacturing decisions.

Before proceeding to a detailed discussion on the new measures to support the new manufacturing operation, it is helpful to briefly review the mindset, the measures, and the methods that characterize the lean, or synchronous, organization.

THE SYNCHRONOUS MINDSET

Research into the best practices of manufacturing companies that have embraced synchronous management shows that these organizations have created a new mindset to counter the mass production mindset. This new mindset is manifested in a new set of behaviors and processes. Companies that have embraced the new mindset do four things well:

1. **They pay attention to what their customers want and work hard to define and deliver it.**

   In the mass production mindset, internal budgets drive daily activities; customer expectations are poorly known (by the rank and file), and expediting is the key customer-driven activity. In most manufacturing companies, there are clear indications of the old mindset at work.

   For instance, the foreman or supervisor's first concern when he or she comes to work is to make sure that all of the operators are assigned some work. This ensures that budgeted production targets will be met. But it does not necessarily mean that the jobs required to meet customer needs are currently in progress.

   Companies that operate under the new mindset show a shift in priority from meeting internal control needs to understanding and satisfying customer needs.

   In a company with a strong customer orientation, the supervisor's first priority is to clearly identify what jobs are needed to meet customer requirements, and to make sure that everyone is working toward accomplishing this. In the leading-

edge companies, the shop floor team understands the company's goals and objectives and how the team's work is linked to the entire organization and its customers.

We call this attribute **customer orientation.**

2. **They work internally to improve the flow of goods and services to those customer requirements.**

The traditional mindset is internal to the point that it becomes local. Each individual/work center is expected to perform to its own best potential (local optimization), in the expectation that this will result in global optimization. But in today's interdependent and unpredictable world of manufacturing this is not true.

Under the traditional mindset, it is common practice to group work at work centers to maximize production efficiencies at each local area. The impact of this grouping on total material flow is of secondary concern, if it is of any concern at all. Most often, attempts to optimize locally have a negative impact on the overall flow of material.

Today's successful companies focus on the global flow of materials — from the suppliers of raw materials and components through the various processes all the way to the customer. Employees share a common understanding of what their product flow is, how it performs today, and the location of major constraints to improvement. The needs of global flow supersede the needs of local optimization in all circumstances.

We call this attribute **material flow orientation.**

3. **They develop flexible and cross-functional organizational structures to promote rapid flow of products and services to the customer.**

The traditional view is that people are to be fully occupied while performing specialized tasks. A hierarchical command-and-control structure organized along functional lines is the norm. Information is made available on a "need-to-know" basis, and individual responsibility consists of executing repetitive tasks within well-defined policy guidelines. Local optimization according to local measures is the objective at department, plant or divisional level. Cross-functional communication is practically non-existent, seriously impeding the flow of information and product to satisfy customer needs.

Successful companies are realigning their organizations to place greater emphasis on promoting product flow all the way from suppliers to the customer. At the heart of the new manufacturing company are cross-functional teams of trained, self-directed and empowered employees charged with providing superior customer service. Managers are required to do less "supervising" and do more "coaching." Employees are required to continuously modify their tasks to make improvements, deliberately changing their jobs rather than following job descriptions without question. Teams are flexible to accommodate the changing day-to-day workloads.

We call this the **customer-aligned organization.**

4. **They consistently seek to achieve the next level of overall performance.**

   In companies who have successfully shifted their internal priorities toward satisfying their customers, improvements are evaluated from the point of view of the customer (Do they add value for the customer?). Everyone is responsible for improving the work flow through his or her area. Small-step improvements are performed by everyone, everywhere, all the time. Unerring focus on the customer is the method for improving competitive position.

   We call this attribute **continuous improvement.**

The difference between the traditional and synchronous mindsets can best be described by the primary focus of an organization or individual exhibiting this mindset. The focus of the traditional mass production mindset is internal and is captured by the phrase:

"Manufacturing is an efficiency machine."

The new synchronous mindset is focused on winning and retaining customers and is captured by the phrase:

"Manufacturing is a sales driver."

SYNCHRONOUS MEASURES

Much of our previous writing *(Regaining Competitiveness: Putting 'The Goal' to Work[3]* and *Synchronous Manufacturing: Principles for World-Class Excellence[1])* was devoted to discussing an alternative system of measuring material flow management and planning that would be free of the shortcomings of the traditional cost system. At that time the focus was on replacing measures based on the local cost system with measures that looked at the entire production operation. Customer focus measures came later and are discussed in chapters 3 and 4 of this book.

Following the work of Dr. Goldratt, a new set of operational measures (Throughput, Inventory, and Operating Expense [T, I, and OE]) were introduced.[2] The abbreviated definitions of these basic terms are listed below. It should be noted that our definitions vary somewhat from Goldratt's. Chapter 5 expands on these definitions and contains examples of their use.

Throughput: The net revenue generated by the company through sales over a specified period of time.

Inventory: The money invested in materials that the company intends to sell.

Operating Expense: The money spent in converting inventory into throughput.

These operational measures overcome the direct labor myopia and the tendency for local optimization of the traditional standard cost system in measuring manufacturing operations. These operational measures have three important characteristics:

1. They are linked to financial success.
2. They evaluate the product flow as a whole.
3. They are intrinsic to the manufacturing process.

In the standard cost system, the business goal of making money translates to the statement that reducing costs generates more profits. In the synchronous view, the objective of making money translates to increasing throughput, reducing inventory, and reducing operating expense, all at the same time. Manufacturing decisions, from batch sizes to new equipment to sourcing, are made by analyzing the impact on all three variables: throughput, inventory, and operating expense.

SYNCHRONOUS METHODS

The methods for managing resources and materials in a manufacturing operation should follow from the mindset that "manufacturing is a sales driver." This means they should support a lean mode of production, the principles of which are fundamentally different from those that govern the traditional mass production which is a high-activity, low-unit-cost mode of production. These principles were introduced in *The Goal*[2] and discussed at length in the book *Synchronous Manufacturing: Principles for World-Class Excellence*[1] and are summarized in Figure 2-2.

Two basic phenomena — **dependent events** and **statistical fluctuations** — are common to all manufacturing operations. The simultaneous presence of both of these phenomena in a manufacturing environment has a very serious consequence. Dependent events occur because of the necessarily sequential nature of production operations. And because of the existence of dependent events, variances in the product flow caused by fluctuations do not average out. Instead, the negative variances accumulate, disrupting the planned product flow for the entire plant (Principle 1).

A manufacturing operation in which production capacity at every step in the process is perfectly balanced with demand is considered the ideal situation in the traditional view. In reality, however, it is virtually impossible to balance the capacity of

Figure 2-2

Synchronous management principles and their traditional equivalents.

	Synchronous Principle	**Traditional Equivalent**
Principle 1	Deviations and disruptions to schedules accumulate at each step. They do not average out.	Deviations and disruptions are contained within the steps in which they occur. Variations will average out over time.
Principle 2	Focus on balancing flow, not capacity.	Focus on balancing capacity. A balanced plant is the ideal condition.
Principle 3	Marginal value of time at a bottleneck resource is equal to the throughput rate of the products processed by the bottleneck. Marginal value of time at a non-bottleneck resource is negligible.	Marginal values will be comparable and have no relationship to capacity. The standard cost system assigns values to both bottlenecks and non-bottlenecks using the same method.
Principle 4	Level of utilization of a non-bottleneck resource is controlled by other constraints of the system.	Utilization of resources can be controlled locally and is based on their potential capability.
Principle 5	Resources contribute to making money only when they are used to make products that can be sold quickly.	Resources contribute to making money by being efficient, by converting as much available time as possible to production time.

resources in a manufacturing plant. Because of the constant occurrence of disruptions, attempts to balance a plant's capacity are often counterproductive. In fact, many activities aimed at balancing capacity may eventually affect T, I, and OE adversely (Principle 2).

Recognizing that we have varying levels of capacity throughout a manufacturing operation allows us to differentiate between two different categories of resources — **bottlenecks** and **non-bottlenecks.** All of the capacity at bottleneck resources is required to meet customer needs. There can be no lost time at a bottleneck, or throughput will suffer. But non-bottleneck resources have some excess capacity. As a result, the marginal value of processing capacity at a bottleneck is extremely valuable, but the marginal value of processing capacity at a non-bottleneck resource is essentially zero (Principles 3 and 4).

Whether a resource is a bottleneck or non-bottleneck makes a significant difference in the impact that it has on material flow, and in the way the resource should be managed. Yet the traditional system is completely ignorant of the difference between bottlenecks and non-bottlenecks. It treats all resources as if they were bottlenecks.

The distinction between different types of resources also leads to the conclusion that there is a distinct difference between the **activation** and the **utilization** of resources. In many cases it is possible to activate a resource, especially a non-bottleneck, beyond what is useful or productive for the total plant. Clearly, resources must only be utilized (activated to contribute positively to the performance of the business as a whole), not simply activated (Principle 5).

The level of utilization that is possible for a non-bottleneck resource is limited by the system constraints. Activating a resource beyond utilization requirements is both wasteful and costly. Yet the traditional focus on efficiency, earned hours, labor productivity, etc., encourages activation as a goal in itself.

Together, the new rules mean that in the highly interdependent world of manufacturing, **ensuring local optimums may not ensure global optimum.** The assumption that local optimums will result in global optimum is at the heart of the traditional approach.

Based on this understanding of production operations, and on the proper understanding of the system's goals (increase T, reduce I, and reduce OE), the material control system described as the Drum-Buffer-Rope (DBR) system was developed. The DBR system provides a product flow that is manageable and that can accommodate the disruptions inherent in every manufacturing process.

The **drum** is the process used to establish the master production schedule for the plant. This process includes modifying a preliminary production plan according to the scheduling requirements of the plant's constrained resources. By doing this, the master production schedule is defined by, and becomes a function of, both market demand and of those resources within the system that constrain production. Thus the demand and the processing capabilities of the most limiting resources determine the pace and production sequence for the entire plant, and the master production schedule becomes the drum beat for the plant.

Buffers refer to time and/or stock buffers (at minimal inventory costs) that are put in place at a few critical points in the process to protect system throughput from both internal fluctuations and external or demand fluctuations. The nature, location, and size of each buffer depends on the detailed nature of the process flow and the customer requirements that need to be met. The key is to have the minimum inventory at strategic locations for maximum protection. Analysis of the buffers can identify and focus both policy and process improvements that can be undertaken to further minimize the buffers.

The **rope** is the last element in the DBR system. The rope provides effective communication of actions that are required to support the master production schedule throughout the operation. Every aspect of the operation must be synchronized to the requirements of the master production schedule so that the planned product flow may be executed. The logistical ropes act to directly link material release and the constraint's production to the master production schedule.

NEW MEASURES ARE REQUIRED FOR
NEW METHODS TO TAKE HOLD

To succeed in the competitive, global markets of today, a manufacturer must change how production is organized and managed. This has been clear for some time. But the type of changes that are required for success cannot be accomplished effectively, unless the measures that guide the decision making process in manufacturing companies are also changed. To use the language of mindset, measures, and methods, the key objective of the new measures is to maintain methods in alignment with customer needs and company objectives. If measures, which are used as decision making tools, are not changed, then the old set of measures will force the new methods to lose effectiveness very quickly.

A clear indication that the old decision making tool needs to be replaced in an organization can be obtained by a simple experiment. Ask the engineers in any organization what criteria they would use to make a purchasing decision between two machines, both capable of meeting production needs. One machine is newer, automated, runs faster, and is more expensive. The other machine is older, rebuilt, and less expensive. If their answer favors the more expensive machine because it lowers labor cost per unit and offers a faster pay back, then it is apparent that their decision making process is still rooted in the old mindset and needs to be realigned.

As another example, if a company has two products which have profit margins of $3 per unit and $2 per unit respectively, which product would the sales representatives push? Would their answer change if the lower "margin" product could be made twice as fast at the bottleneck resource?

As noted at the beginning of this chapter, effective organizational change involves modifying each of the three M's: Mindset, Measures and Methods. The technology of synchronous management is oriented toward developing a self-consistent approach to addressing all three elements. The focus of discussions in this book is "measures." A key objective of the In-Sync set of measures developed in the rest of this book is to assist all members of the organization in making valid business decisions. These decisions must be supported, in turn, by appropriate operating methods and mindset.

CHAPTER 3

IN-SYNC
A BALANCED
AND STRUCTURED SET

In a fiercely competitive and global market, manufacturing companies need to address a host of competitive elements. It is not enough to simply manufacture a product with high internal efficiencies.

It follows that it is no longer sufficient to measure the single dimension of cost. While most manufacturing managers understand this intuitively, they continue to use traditional manufacturing measurements that evaluate internal operating efficiencies with great precision and place great importance on these traditional measures.

Measurement systems must be expanded to include critical factors for success in a competitive market. These measurements must evaluate how satisfied current customers are with the company's performance, how the company is performing relative to the competition, and how the company is performing financially. Establishing appropriate performance measures for these elements is a key to success.

Measurement systems are a powerful tool to communicate priorities and guide decision making. Management must communicate to the organization the performance of the business and also identify the key performance improvements that are needed. Implicit in the synchronous approach is the concept of constraint identification and management. Measures for managing constraints will provide specific detailed information to improve the performance of the constraints and, hence, that of the entire business.

In most organizations, there is no shortage of indicators that are measured, tabulated, charted, displayed and/or reviewed by someone. This is a natural outgrowth of the recognition over the last two decades that labor efficiency alone does not present the complete picture. The problem today is not that companies don't measure enough, but that they measure too many things. For example, one large company measured and intended to review fifty key measures every week. Not one of these measures evaluated the manufacturing organization from an external perspective. They were all intended to optimize various internal parameters, which in turn would have fine tuned the cost to produce parts.

Often, the items measured are not part of a coherent framework. Measures, such as labor efficiency and inventory level, are in conflict with each other. The efficiency mindset is pervasive and affects all items measured. Quality, for example, is often measured by its impact on labor hours earned (or labor efficiency) rather than by its impact on customers or competitive position. Measuring the number of hours of rework done, and allocating the negative impact to the department doing the rework reflects the old mindset. Measuring the number or value of customer orders that need rework, and allocating responsibility to the department causing the need for rework reflects a healthier approach.

In devising a new set of measures, we are attempting to replace the many disparate items (measured by different groups, different sections, and different levels of an organization) with a single comprehensive set of measures. This set of measures must be multi-dimensional; it cannot be totally financial in nature, but must also reflect customer satisfaction and competitive position.

It is necessary here to clear up a key point that causes confusion when discussing the topic of accounting systems and operational measures. The objective of our structured set of measures is not to provide a new means for financial reporting, but to provide the tools for operational decision making. Financial reporting must be done according to accepted standards. Companies, however, need not continue to use yesterday's systems when making today's decisions.

We refer to our balanced and structured set of measures as the **In-Sync** set.

THE GROUPS WITHIN THE IN-SYNC SET

There are a few important design criteria for any specific set of measures for a company's manufacturing operation.

1. **External Customer Focus:** In a buyers' market, an external view is a matter of survival. Numerous competitive elements must be addressed, such as product, quality, delivery reliability, lead time, and price. The elements that are important to a company's customers must be identified. These must then be defined as the customers define them, not as the seller would like to define them.

   A simple example of this distinction is provided in measuring delivery performance. The supplier would like to measure deliveries against the promise date and not the original customer request date (which may be deemed totally unreasonable).

But customers are really measuring the supplier to their (the customers') request date!

2. **Internal Focus On Making Money:** An internal focus on making money is a financial necessity. If managers are to make improvements that will result in the company making more money over time, then manufacturing measures need to be directly linked to financial performance. It is widely acknowledged that the bridge between operational performance measures and financial performance is not cost accounting, with its focus on labor efficiency (see *Relevance Lost: The Rise and Fall Of Management Accounting*[4] and *Synchronous Manufacturing: Principles for World-Class Excellence*[1]). The challenge is to articulate a set of measures that does create this bridge in a simple and effective manner.

3. **Structure and Balance:** No single measure can drive improvements. Only a structured set of measures and a balanced management interpretation can do that.

There are four groups within the structured set of manufacturing measurements. As shown in Figure 3-1, two are external — customer satisfaction and competitive position. The other two are internal — operational performance and what we call the local indicators.

Customer Satisfaction relates to how satisfied current customers are with the company's products and services.

Competitive Position refers to how the company's products and services are seen by customers and non-customers alike, relative to competitors.

Figure 3-1

Groups within the In-Sync measures set and their major focus.

Orientation	Measure	Key Question Addressed
External	Customer Satisfaction	What do customers expect? Are the customers happy?
	Competitive Position	Where is the company relative to the competition?
Internal	Operational Performance	How well is the company managing its assets?
	Local Indicators	Which specific aspect of the operation needs improvement?

Operational performance relates to the effectiveness with which manufacturing assets are managed. In synchronous management these are measured by Throughput, Inventory, and Operating Expense.

Local indicators are measurements of individual activities that help evaluate how those activities are affecting customer satisfaction, competitive position and global corporate profitability. These measures help relate specific local activities to the performance of the entire business.

We believe that each company must measure performance using all four groups of measurements. However, within each group, there are a number of different possible measures, the details of which will vary by circumstance.

Figure 3-2 shows the relationship between the global objective of making money and the structured set of measures. The external measures are focused on driving the volume of business up. The internal measures are designed to assist in driving the relative level of spending down. The local indicators provide the detailed information necessary to identify specific improvements/changes that can help improve external or internal measures.

It should be pointed out that while the changes in market conditions have made the balanced measurement system a must, it is a good idea even in a sellers' market to maintain a customer focus. This can enable the manufacturer to win additional market share.

Figure 3-2
Relationship between the In-Sync measures and the financial measures.

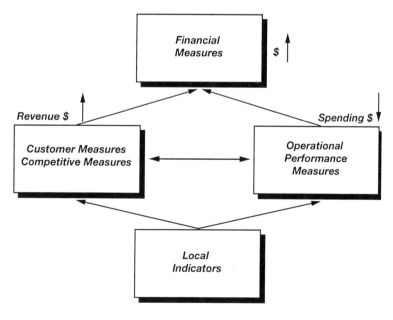

In summary, the traditional measures are rooted in the mass production mindset that **manufacturing is an efficiency machine.** As shown in Figure 3-3, the measures reinforce this mindset by measuring and tracking direct labor activity.   By design, measures play the critical role of aligning methods with mindset.   It is no coincidence that mass production methods are directed at improving labor efficiency.   By contrast, the In-Sync measures are rooted in the mindset that **manufacturing is a sales driver.** As shown in Figure 3-3, the In-Sync set measures customer satisfaction, total sales and total spending. Synchronous methods are thus directed at improving competitive position and profits.

Figure 3-3

Comparison of traditional and synchronous approaches showing how mindset determines the measures and, in turn, the methods.

	Traditional View	Synchronous View
Mindset	Manufacturing is a cost driver.	Manufacturing is a sales driver.
What is paramount	Control costs and labor efficiency.	Increase sales and control spending.
What gets measured	Direct labor activity.	Throughput and operating expenses; total sales and total spending.
What gets done	Drives activation to increase labor efficiency.	Drives utilization to improve competitive elements and total spending.

CUSTOMER (EXTERNAL) MEASURES -
THE STARTING POINT

The basic need in a business is to assure that there is a steady flow of revenue from satisfied customers. Hence the critical question that must be constantly asked is:

What do we need to improve so that customers will buy more of and pay more for our products and services?

In the buyers' market, the critical issue is not simply price. Instead, there are a host of prerequisites a company must have in order to compete. Time and again, when we ask clients how they choose suppliers, the response is: "They (the suppliers) need to have a, b, c, d and e attributes. That gets them on the short list. Then we haggle over price."

Customers are demanding perfect delivery, just-in-time, at parts-per-million quality, before they even ask about the price. Demand fluctuates in volume and mix, which puts a further premium on flexibility and responsiveness.

Because of this, a company needs to establish its customer focus measures as drivers. Getting answers to basic questions about customer desires, needs and satisfaction, both with the company's product and with competitors' products, will help determine the internal measures that will drive operations.

These measures will expose both the customer's current "hot buttons" and the present level of customer satisfaction. They also should indicate a customer's future hot buttons, which will help determine what can be done to boost competitive position in the future.

A good start is to rank order the five attributes customers are increasingly considering as the "price of admission" to making the short list of potential suppliers (before price is even discussed):

  product features
  delivery reliability
  lead time
  quality
  service

From these externally focused measures one can begin to design a set of measures that will drive improvement in the areas that were highlighted.   Chapter 4 addresses this issue in more detail.

INTERNAL MEASURES - QUESTION OF PROFITABILITY

The next key issue is operational effectiveness.   The measures of operational performance must relate to the three standard measures of financial success — net profit, return on investment, and cash flow.   These measures are, however, difficult to translate into measures or indicators on the shop floor.

While it may be relatively easy for the vice president of manufacturing to understand how the actions he or she takes equate to the balance sheet and income statement, that is not necessarily true for the plant manager, the shop supervisor, the machine operator or the manufacturing engineer.

The traditional link between the local actions of these manufacturing personnel and the company's global financial performance was thought to be the standard cost system.   But (as we have highlighted in the discussion of synchronous management methods in chapter 2) this is not a valid indicator of whether manufacturing performance equates to corporate financial performance.

A much clearer link from shop floor operational performance to corporate financial performance can be found in a framework for measuring operations using the three simple measures discussed in chapter 2:

- Throughput (T)
- Inventory (I)
- Operating Expense (OE)

In the old system, it was easy to see if each level of the manufacturing organization was making more money simply by looking at the labor efficiency and the unit costs of a part produced. It was assumed that if productivity was going up — defined in the old way as *more activity with the same or less resources* — then the company was making more money.

In reality, it doesn't matter how much is being **produced**; it must be **sold** to generate revenue. Instead of linking actions to the amount of material produced or activity generated, as the standard cost system does, using T, I, OE measures links actions to the amount sold. The difference is subtle but profound.

Also, T, I, and OE measures encompass all of the spending under a manager's control, not just the direct labor force. This will encourage a balance between labor reduction and reduction in the other elements of cost (such as scrap, inventory, overtime, offloading). As part of the overall set, these measures keep in perspective both improvements in the competitive elements and labor cost reductions. Simple labor cost reduction often hinders improvement in some competitive elements. Finally, T, I, and OE measures encourage speed and flexibility, which are becoming increasingly important in today's highly competitive environment.

USING THE NEW GLOBAL MEASURES

The objective of managerial decisions is to have T increasing while I and OE are decreasing. This can't always happen, but these measures allow for the calculation of any set of potential tradeoffs. Evaluating tradeoffs using the standard cost system versus using the global measures — external and T, I, and OE — usually results in very different conclusions.

Consider the case where two setup workers are hired in order to reduce the changeover time at a critical work center by 75 percent. A cost-based analysis would compare the additional cost of the new employees — let's say $30,000 each — with the savings in setup time — let's say 1,500 hours annually at $30 per hour. Clearly, the cost ($60,000) outweighs the savings ($45,000).

An In-Sync analysis would ask what "value" can be provided to the customer with the reduced setup times that would make the customer decide to purchase more from the company. If the reduced setup time can be translated into lead time reductions of 50 percent, then responsiveness to customer demands has been improved. This should provide a competitive advantage.

Let us assume that such responsiveness could generate an extra 5 percent in sales for a $10 million business. This additional sales would require only a marginal increase in capacity and in the purchase of additional material. If material makes up a typical 40% of the sales price, then Throughput would increase by $300,000 (Since T = sales minus material price). This would be accomplished with minimal change in Inventory, and with Operating Expenses increasing by the cost of the two additional workers (or $60,000). The evaluation is now quite different.

Figure 3-4
Matrix to evaluate the impact of various productivity initiatives on the competitive factors.

Impact Matrix	Measure	
Attribute or Program	**Total Expenses**	**Competitive Position**
Higher labor flexibility		
Availability of excess capacity		
Preventive Maintenance		
Zero Defects		
One piece lots		

THE NEED FOR BALANCE

Figure 3-4 shows a number of improvement activities or programs, such as improved labor flexibility (through cross-training), preventive maintenance programs, zero defects, and one piece lots. Each of these programs will have an effect on both the customer satisfaction measures and the internal operational measures. Most of these programs show a negative impact on standard cost system measures such as unit cost. In fact, this is the reason that many of these programs were not implemented in the past.

Managers are frustrated by the inability of the standard cost system to support actions they intuitively feel to be correct. It would seem obvious that efforts such as preventive maintenance are the proper thing to do. Yet the standard cost system calculations indicate otherwise. It overvalues the time lost while maintenance is performed and undervalues the benefits of eliminating the disruptive downtimes.

The right things may eventually get done, but time is lost, and the effort is half-hearted. The In-Sync set evaluates these same efforts in terms of their impact on customer satisfaction and future sales. Changes in throughput, and the cumulative impact of reducing equipment downtimes on current expenses are offset by any additional expenses incurred in implementing the program. The balanced consideration of these elements provides the justification for the effort.

Consider, for example, the drive for one-piece lots or for "zero inventory." When getting started with batch size and lead time reductions, the initial activities under this program will have a positive effect on both external and internal In-Sync measures. The initial changes can be implemented with minimal changes in tooling, equipment, training, etc.

These minimal expenditures will be more than offset by gains in inventory, quality, and so on. Total expenses will, in all likelihood, decrease. Lead times and delivery performance measures will improve.

As the batch size reduction program continues, a point will eventually be reached where additional reductions will require significant expenditures to modify equipment and/or processes. The additional reductions in lead time and/or delivery performance will have to be compared against the increase in expenses, in order to determine whether to pursue the batch size reduction. The benefit of reducing batch size from four to one, in terms of additional sales due to increased responsiveness, may be minimal. The expense required to achieve the batch size reduction, in terms of new tools, fixtures, employee training, etc., could be substantial.

At this point, batch size reduction can not be justified according to the In-Sync measures. Simply stated, batch size reduction is a means to achieving the business goal. The benefits on the customer side and the resulting additional sales will have to be carefully weighed against real increases in expenses.

The **value** of customer measures and operational measures of T, I, and OE is that they are globally rather than locally-focused. In the standard cost framework, savings resulting from a particular action were assumed to translate to savings for the entire plant. This is a faulty assumption. Within the synchronous measurement system, cost savings in and of themselves are not the primary focus. Instead, the question is whether the activity — anything from buying a new machine to consolidating lines — has a positive or negative impact on each of the external measures and on the three operational measures, and the tradeoffs involved.

LOCAL INDICATORS

The measures discussed so far — customer, competitive and operational — help to identify whether a company is winning or losing the game of manufacturing and also serve to highlight those elements that need improvement. The analogous situation in a football game is to know how many points a team has scored, how many points they have allowed, and which major area of the game is a weakness. The score in itself does not identify what needs improving. More detailed measures are needed to help identify the specific area (such as run offense) needing improvement.

A key concept of the synchronous management approach is that of constraints. By definition, constraints limit the performance of any organization. Ensuring proper management of constraints is critical if the organization is to achieve optimum performance. The measures that help manage and control the performance of the constraint to the best advantage of the entire business are called **constraint measures.** For example, if material availability is the constraint then the constraint measure would be the yield for this material through the process.

To underscore the important role of constraints and provide crucial managerial focus, we have elevated the constraint measure to a "global" measure. The In-Sync set for the business will hence include the customer-based measures, the operational measures based on T, I, OE, and the constraint measures. By reviewing both the global performance measures and the constraint measures, management will be reviewing both the overall score and the critical areas that must be most closely controlled for the performance of the entire unit to be optimized.

The In-Sync set described above works at the level of the entire business. But what about sub-units (in the case of large organizations) and individual work centers and individual activities? For the new methods to take hold, they cannot continue to operate under the guidance of the old standard cost system. We need to develop a replacement set of measures for sub-units as well as for individual activities.

The customer-based and operational measures at the business level provide information on how well the business is performing. The measures that help evaluate performance of individual activities are called **local indicators** or **local measures**. Appropriately constructed local indicators must help relate local activities to overall business performance. Otherwise, the result of improving local performance as measured by these indicators will result in sub-optimization. While it is a simple and necessary requirement to insist that local indicators be tied to total system performance, this is difficult to achieve in practice. This is where the techniques of synchronous management would be most useful. We call these local indicators **activity-outcome measures.**

Consider a department that provides two components, both of which are required at a subsequent assembly operation. The number of matched sets produced would be an example of an activity-outcome measure. Simply counting the number of units produced (or the equivalent standard hours) would not be a good activity-outcome measure, since a unit without its matching component would be useless.

It is safe to say that every aspect of every activity can be made better. However, a basic tenet of synchronous management is that in the complex world of manufacturing every improvement does not have the same impact on the entire business. To leverage improvement activities, everyone must answer the question:

What specific area, aspect or process within our span of control do we need to improve to achieve maximum impact on the entire business?

Clearly, the answer will change with each individual and each sub-unit. At the level of the president, the answer leads to the constraints of the business. The measures that help manage and control the performance of the constraint to the best advantage of the entire business are, of course, the constraint measures.

At the level of an individual operator, he or she must identify what aspect of his/her performance has the most impact on the business. This is equivalent to identifying the activity-outcome measure the improvement of which will help the business the most. The measures that help manage this specific activity so that the critical activity-outcome measure improves are called **activity-focusing measures.**

The development of local indicators (or activity-outcome measures) and activity-focusing measures complete the In-Sync set of measures. As represented in Figure 3-2, the business objective of making money remains the one clear goal. One needs to make sure customers are satisfied and that one manages assets effectively. The customer and operational measures are designed to provide information regarding the organization's performance relative to these two items. Finally, local indicators provide detailed and local information to assist everyone in the organization (from top management to engineers to shop floor operators) do the best they can and engage in relevant and focused improvement activities.

CHAPTER 4

CUSTOMER FOCUS MEASURES

In a buyers' market, manufacturing organizations must be focused on continually growing market share and on increasing the relative level of throughput. The only way to accomplish this effectively is to look beyond the four walls of the factory and to truly understand the customer's performance requirements.

As obvious as this may seem, this is one of the more difficult changes to accomplish in any company. Most of the measures traditionally used have very little to do with external, customer-related items. While every facet of labor costs and other cost elements have been measured to minute levels of detail, even rudimentary information regarding shipments, lead times, etc. are generally not available. Performance to budget has been the holy grail of operations managers, while performance to customer expectations has only appeared on the "radar screen" lately.

While some managers have started measuring items that relate to the question of customer satisfaction, few have actually made the mindset shift required by current market conditions. Without the mindset change, the danger is always present that even items that purport to measure customer satisfaction subconsciously become modified to measure production efficiency. As factors that are believed important to the customer are identified and definitions and tracking systems are developed, one must make continuous and rigorous efforts to be sure these factors remain truly customer-focused.

In this context, "the customer" can be taken to mean the next-level user for whom the product is made. For some operations this means the ultimate consumer of a product or service. For others this means a sister division that assembles or transforms the product further. If each element in the supply chain is focused on the requirements of the next-level user as though they are the customer, ultimately the final customer will be served.

In a buyers' market, customers are demanding that producers meet a threshold level of performance on an increasing number of attributes. Once the minimum level has been met, the discussion on price/cost generally begins. For most customers the short list of attributes includes:

- product features
- delivery reliability
- lead time
- quality
- service

This list is longer in some industries and markets, but rarely shorter. It's not enough to understand that these are the cutomers' "hot buttons" for a particular company. They are customers' "hot buttons" for all companies; they are the prerequisites that must be met before price is even discussed.

Consider the criteria an individual uses in making purchasing decisions. Whether the individual is purchasing an automobile or a major household appliance, the elements listed above are the deciding issues. This same purchasing criteria holds true in institutional buying decisions as well. When a potential buyer goes to a specific automobile dealership he or she looks for certain attributes. He is interested in a specific model of car which has the features, styling and reputation for quality at the price he is willing to pay. The dealer must also have the ability to deliver the car in an acceptable time frame and to provide after-sale service.

Depending on the nature of the individual purchase, one or two of these attributes may be more important than the others. Even if a specific automobile doesn't have the best fuel economy, its styling may be attractive enough to sway the buyer's decision anyway. Different competitive elements will carry more weight than others. The same holds true with respect to organizational purchasing decisions. Certain suppliers may have specific technological advantages, but their delivery performance may be poor. Buying decisions are complex yet the same fundamental elements are always at work.

What changes from customer to customer, or from product to product, is the relative priority attached to each element. This is generally product or market sensitive. If these attributes are to be effectively used to win new customers and do more business with current customers, then it must be understood how customers (current and future) rank these attributes in level of importance.

We call these performance attributes **the competitive elements**, or the *competitive imperatives*.

The purpose of understanding a customer's needs (within the context of developing a comprehensive set of performance measures) is primarily to provide focus in determining what measures to employ. Secondarily, it gives the various measures relative priority. The competitive elements, while having significant implications from an internal financial perspective, relate specifically to external performance attributes.

DETERMINING WHAT IS "MOST" IMPORTANT

Developing an understanding of what customers think are the most important attributes can be a long and expensive process, or it can be done more quickly and less expensively. And as is often the case, the more time, effort and money put into the exercise the more reliable the data. Many organizations utilize outside research or consulting groups to gather and interpret this data, although this is certainly not necessary as a starting point.

For most companies, a quick and relatively inexpensive effort can at least create a baseline from which it is possible to both formulate and focus performance measurement criteria.

The focus in this exercise is merely to understand what customers want and need from the products and services they buy. Determining where a company's products and services fall with regard to competitors is the next level of detail. Although both are important, it is our belief that the customer information should precede the competitor survey. If a customer's perceptions can be understood with reasonable accuracy, a more focused and effective competitor ranking can be achieved.

Determining customer desires and determining competitive position are really two sides of the same coin. It must be assumed that one's competitors are doing an equivalent amount of research and analysis.

One needs to focus on what one can do to give *today's* customers what they want and desire, regardless of what the competitive analysis reveals about the relative position of competitors. Yet, at the same time, one needs to find a way to determine what the customer will want in the future. Being first to the marketplace with the right combination of attributes will provide a distinct competitive advantage.

We like to think about the difference between customer focus and competitive position as the difference between focusing on what a company can do today to meet customers' needs and desires, and what a company should do in the future to gain and maintain a competitive advantage.

At this point, it is important to highlight that there often exists significant discrepancies between *perceived* customer wants and needs and *actual* customer wants and needs. For this reason, it is important at the outset of developing a new performance measurement set to question assumptions and to develop some hard data.

Too often we have encountered organizations acting on assumptions, not facts, concerning the customer. This situation is usually attributable to the chasm that exists between the sales, marketing, and manufacturing groups. Functionally organized companies traditionally have communication problems in this specific area. Occasionally the relationship between sales and manufacturing is actually antagonistic, which further undermines the reliability of manufacturing's assumptions about the external marketplace.

Perhaps a good starting place for any company rethinking its measurement set is to evaluate the level and quality of current communications and to begin making organizational and structural changes to facilitate the sales-to-manufacturing linkage. The level of integration achieved between the sales and manufacturing functions has a direct relationship to the amount of customer focus brought to the shop floor. In this competitive environment it is a fact of business life that these two functions must be mutually supportive. A key concept in synchronous management is the notion of manufacturing as a sales driver. All too often manufacturing is looked upon as a necessary evil, rather than as a way to leverage improvements in garnering greater market share.

The exercises we will go through in this chapter focus on evaluating the current business and developing a true understanding of customers' needs and desires.

DEVELOPING THE DATA

A primary source of information relating to customer concerns is the sales staff. What vital information has the sales staff acquired during sales calls? In addition to finding out what the "key" attribute or attributes are in the marketplace, a company needs to find out why people buy from them as opposed to their competitors, and why the company at times loses business. Remember, at this point rigorous comparisons between the company and particular competitors is not what is needed; the company merely needs to understand what it is the marketplace requires.

One way a company can accomplish this effectively is to perform an analysis of the bids *lost* over the past year. The salespeople responsible for each bid can be interviewed in an attempt to identify the specific criteria the company failed to meet.

In performing this analysis, trends are likely to emerge that should help to rank order the competitive elements in the marketplace. The logic behind examining lost bids as opposed to successful ones is that there is likely to be a myriad of reasons why a client places an order, while the reasons for rejection are usually quite specific. The idea here is to develop a focused understanding of where manufacturing operations are falling short.

Another approach is to conduct a service survey of the current customer base as well as potential customers. This is often time-consuming and can be expensive, but direct feedback from customer decision makers is obviously the best source of information. The survey should be constructed carefully to ensure objective feedback, and the respondents should be selectively chosen. The data derived from this type of effort is often quite surprising, and again should help determine the relative priority of the specific performance measurement criteria to be used internally.

Figure 4-1

Which performance attribute is most important today and in the future?

Performance Attribute Ranking Matrix		
Performance Attribute	**Important Today**	**Important In The Future**
Cycle Time		
Delivery Performance		
Quality		
Product Features		
Service		
Price		

Key: 1 = most important, 5 = least important

A, B, or C rankings may be assigned to each attribute, or they may be ranked numerically with 1 representing the most important attribute to the customer base. The results are typically tabulated as shown in Figure 4-1.

From these rankings, combined with an understanding of what a company does well, one can determine more accurately how to construct the measurement set, as well as the effort needed to improve particular attributes. This can be shown as a percentage of resources devoted to improving each attribute, or by ranking the attributes in the order in which the improvement effort will be focused.

For instance, consider the case of Company XYZ, a manufacturer of products for high technology applications. For years, the management team's focus had been on the engineering and technology aspects of the company's products. Company XYZ believed that it was successful and that customers bought from them because of superior technology.

The reality of the situation was that the customer base was much more interested in the delivery and cost elements than in the engineering technology. But rather than focus resources and management attention on these elements, the manufacturing organization continued to devote disproportionate levels of time and effort on the technical aspect.

As the situation evolved, this company saw its market share erode at an ever increasing rate. Clearly there existed a disconnect between what manufacturing perceived as the critical competitive elements and what the customers really wanted. Finally, an external survey was conducted among customers, with surprising results for the manufacturing management team. Figure 4-2 summarizes the feedback received from customers.

Figure 4-2

Relative importance of Competitive Elements for each customer in the case of company XYZ.

		Competitive Element				
Customer	% Sales	Delivery	Quality	Price	Service	Product
Customer # 1	45%	1	3	2	4	5
Customer # 2	25%	1	3	2	4	5
Customer # 3	10%	1	2	3	4	5
Customer # 4	10%	1	2	3	4	5
Customer # 5	10%	1	3	2	4	5
Total	100%	5	13	12	20	25

Key: 1 = most important, 5 = least important

Clearly, in this example the customer survey technique provided hard data indicating that the manufacturing organization had been focused on the wrong issue relative to maintaining and growing market share.

The survey was used to realign the relative importance of the various competitive elements within the company's production operations, with a corresponding shift in emphasis to delivery performance. The methods and measures used in the plants were changed to support this realignment. The result was that the company recaptured market share and received a positive response from customers, who believed they were finally being heard.

Another aspect of the external survey technique involves asking the customer base to rate the organization relative to its key competitors. The defining criteria remain the same, i.e. the competitive elements. But the emphasis is on where the organization ranks with the competition. Figure 4-3 shows the results received in the same survey.

Figure 4-3
Competitive Position of Company XYZ as ranked by customers.

Competitors	Competitive Element				
	Delivery	Quality	Price	Service	Product
Competitor # 1	3	1	4	5	2
Competitor # 2	1	4	5	3	3
Competitor # 3	2	5	3	1	4
Competitor # 4	4	2	1	2	5
Company XYZ	5	3	2	4	1

Key: 1 = best, 5 = worst

It is obvious, when viewing this information in conjunction with Figure 4-2, to see why the company had lost competitive position and needed to refocus on real customer needs, not perceived customer needs. Again, the overriding theme is to create substantive linkages between the manufacturing and sales/marketing organizations, so that the way that manufacturing is managed reflects market needs and desires. Leveraging manufacturing improvements in critical areas important to the customer is the best way to improve business and ensure positive relationships with customers. The development of performance measures that focus specifically on these critical attributes is one of the most effective ways of achieving this end.

It is also important to understand that this exercise of customer surveys and competitive benchmarking is not a one-time event. Certainly it will be necessary to periodically reevaluate the company's position within the marketplace and to understand how its customer requirements are evolving. As the organization moves forward with the implementation of customer focus measures, customers' perceptions will likely change, thus necessitating periodic recalibration. Most organizations feel the need to review the market's requirements on a semi-annual basis, with a full competitive benchmarking yearly.

Now let us look at how an organization might develop some performance measures that relate specifically to the competitive elements discussed above. It is also important to highlight that none of these elements exists in a vacuum. Clearly the product characteristics element must be viewed in relation to total cost as well as quality. Although the specific measures developed will obviously relate to the industry and markets that an organization services, the following represent some general ideas. The crucial point to remember in choosing or developing the customer focus measures for a business is to understand how customers define these measures. In addition to defining the measures the same way as its customers, a company can stay ahead of the game if it sets more stringent parameters and targets than the customers. A company that defines these measures to suit its own needs is, in effect, putting its head in the sand.

PRODUCT FEATURES / CHARACTERISTICS

This relates to the customers' evaluation of the specific products a company produces *relative* to its competition. Information concerning this does not necessarily relate to the manufacturing function's performance, but rather to the engineering and development aspects. Generally, organizations attempt to balance product cost with product features within the development arena. Obviously, if the customer and competitor surveys indicate a lack of competitiveness in this area the engineering/development side of the business must become involved.

In consumer products in particular, design and product features are critical competitive elements. In the automobile market, for example, tilt steering wheels and anti-lock braking systems (ABS) are product features that all auto manufacturers have been forced to include due to the features' perceived importance by the consumer.

As a performance measure, product features differ from the remaining competitive elements in that performance on this aspect will not be judged on a daily or weekly basis. While every customer order shipped can be judged with regard to timeliness, every order cannot be judged on whether it had all the features desired by the customer or if these features were available from the competition. The comparison of a company's product to competitive products and to known expectations of the target market should be done periodically in a benchmarking-style exercise. The frequency of this comparison will depend on the industry. For the automotive industry, benchmarking every six months may be appropriate; for consumer products such as videocassette recorders (VCR's), three months may be the outside limit between competitive benchmarking activities.

Clearly, in developing the benchmarking exercises and assigning importance to various aspects of product design and features, marketing strategy plays a crucial role. Focus should be placed on those aspects a company expects to exploit in the marketplace. The primary players in this scenario are marketing and design engineering. Manufacturing and process engineering play the crucial role of ensuring manufacturability of the products.

DELIVERY RELIABILITY AND DELIVERY PERFORMANCE

This relates to a company's ability to meet commitments made to customers. It does not necessarily provide a good indication of whether or not the commitments themselves were acceptable; that relates to the lead time discussion below.

For example, delivery reliability measures a company's dependability in meeting a four-week commitment. Yet even if this company is successful in delivering to that four-week commitment, the customer may (unbeknownst to the company) prefer a two-week delivery. If this is the case, it is a safe bet the customer is shopping for alternate suppliers. This simply underscores the point that none of the measures are complete indicators in isolation.

The delivery-reliability time frame utilized should have an appropriate "window," based on the market serviced. By this we mean the tolerance of the marketplace to the dates specified, the "plus or minus" time allowed. It was not long ago that some organizations utilized a "month of" window. If an order was due in January and it was delivered sometime in January, then the order was considered to be on-time. Clearly this window is too wide for the vast majority of businesses today. The narrower the window the more difficult it is to meet. This relates directly to the amount of control and discipline exercised on the shop floor relative to the priority and sequencing of products.

The stringency of this measure should serve to drive the improvement effort in this area. Further, this window must reflect customer expectations, i.e. what do the customers perceive to be on time? As mentioned earlier, a company can stay ahead of the game by making its standards more stringent than its customers'.

While delivery reliability is, in effect, a yes-or-no issue, delivery performance can be measured in a number of different ways. Customer orders may consist of multiple products (or line items) and may be for multiple units of a given product. The order also has a dollar value assigned to it. Figure 4-4 shows sample orders due week 10, and the actual shipments in week 10 against these orders. Based on whether a company chooses to evaluate entire orders, individual line items, total units ordered, or total dollars ordered, different delivery performance numbers will result as shown.

Figure 4-4

Alternative measures of delivery performance.

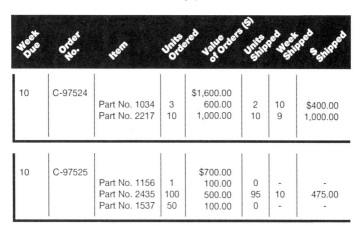

Week Due	Order No.	Item	Units Ordered	Value of Orders ($)	Units Shipped	Week Shipped	$ Shipped
10	C-97524			$1,600.00			
		Part No. 1034	3	600.00	2	10	$400.00
		Part No. 2217	10	1,000.00	10	9	1,000.00
10	C-97525			$700.00			
		Part No. 1156	1	100.00	0	-	-
		Part No. 2435	100	500.00	95	10	475.00
		Part No. 1537	50	100.00	0	-	-

Alternative definition 1:

Delivery performance % = $\dfrac{\text{percent of orders shipped "complete"}}{\text{total number of orders due}}$

= $^{0}/_{2}$ = 0%

Alternative definition 2:

Delivery performance % = $\dfrac{\text{percent of pieces or units shipped on-time or early}}{\text{total number of units due}}$

= $\dfrac{107 \text{ units (on-time or early)}}{164 \text{ units (due)}}$ = 65.2%

Alternative definition 3:

Delivery performance % = $\dfrac{\text{dollars shipped on-time or early}}{\text{total dollars due}}$

= $\dfrac{\$1875 \text{ (on-time)}}{\$2300}$ = 81.5%

The delivery performance measure chosen should reflect how customers measure a supplier.

LEAD TIME

This relates specifically to the lead time quoted to the customer. If the customer orders a product today, when will he receive the product? This is another area where customer feedback will play an essential role in defining the measure. We have seen substantial mismatches between what the customer perceives as the lead time and what the producer believes is the proper lead time. Issues such as transportation time, receiving and inspection time, etc. often lead to misunderstandings concerning the "real" lead time. Alignment in this area is critical if the measure is to be meaningful.

It should also be pointed out that there exists a substantial amount of confusion concerning the use of the terms "lead time" and "cycle time." In our usage, lead time relates to the amount of time quoted to the customer for order fulfillment,

Figure 4-5
Alternative measures of cycle/lead time

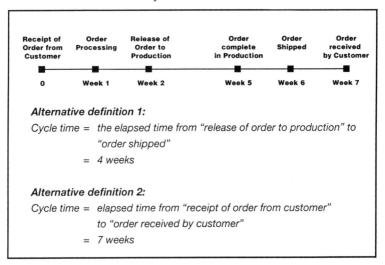

while cycle time relates to the *actual, demonstrated* time to produce the order. Cycle time performance should be measured and analyzed to pinpoint how to improve customer quoted lead times. One of the best places to gather information concerning cycle time is through the shop paperwork, such as routing "cards." This usually contains the start date and the completion date, as well as dates for completion of all the intermediate operations. A statistical sampling of these can provide unique insight into the actual flow of material through the shop.

Figure 4-5 contains some key dates in the life of an order. Depending on which activities start and stop the "cycle time" clock, different values for the cycle time will result. Some of the more frequently used definitions of cycle time and the result of applying that specific definition to the example are also shown. Note that as mentioned above, in our terminology, alternative definition 1 in Figure 4-5 means "cycle time," while alternative definition 2 means "lead time."

It is essential that a company achieve alignment with its customers concerning their expectations and concerning the company's performance. Once this has been done, meaningful statistical measures for each product line can be derived.

QUALITY

Once again, this must be judged in relation to *customer expectations*. The level of these expectations are usually not created by the company, but rather through the competitive interactions of the market itself. In this sense quality is much like cost — there exists a threshold through which a supplier must pass if there is any expectation of doing business at all. This is important to understand because in this area, the company often has to deal with customer *perceptions* rather than what it may consider objective reality. Although the type of measures employed in this area are necessarily industry-specific, there are some basic customer quality measures to which almost everyone can relate.

Delivery performance and lead time can be measured internally. Customer perceptions of quality, however, cannot. The customer has to provide feedback. Customers may do this in very obvious fashion, by returning defective material or by making warranty claims. They may take the time to call a supplier's service department and complain about the quality of product/service. They may fix the defect themselves and not lodge any complaints. Customers may, as is increasingly common today, provide the supplier with performance and ranking information. Whether or not a customer is doing supplier evaluations today, such information should be actively pursued. The onus is on the supplier to actively solicit information relative to quality performance.

Listed below are some of the commonly used measures of quality:

- Number of returns per unit shipped
- Dollar value of returns to dollar value of shipments
- Number of complaints logged per unit shipped
- Number of deviations reported per unit shipped

SERVICE

This is a broad topic under which a variety of elements fall. Areas such as the speed with which complaints are resolved, the speed and cost of repair activities, modes of transportation employed, etc. all relate to what customers perceive as service. An example is the service garage where cars are repaired. One garage might only provide the basic repair service, while another might provide a loaner car, wash and wax the car before returning it, or might even pick up and drop off the customer at his place of work.

These additional services weigh heavily in favor of that garage, yet if its prices are out of line or the quality is missing, that garage would still fail to attract business. Because the perception of service varies so widely by industry it isn't especially useful to provide examples. Customer feedback should provide insight into whether or not an organization is providing the level and type of service required. Complaint resolution, maintenance and repair activities, etc. can then be focused appropriately.

The external, customer-focused measures one develops must be driven from the data acquired *externally*. They do not necessarily relate to budgets, internal goals, etc. The balance achieved through their construct should reflect the relative importance assigned by the customers themselves. Manufacturing has been typically insulated from the customer by sales and marketing. These external measures are the opportunity for the market to actually drive activities and improvement efforts within the organization. This will help to increase market share and profitability.

EXAMPLE OF CUSTOMER FOCUS MEASURES AT THE PLANT LEVEL

We will illustrate the design of the various groups of measures of the In-Sync set in this chapter and in chapters 5, 6, and 7, by using the example of a primary metal manufacturer. Here we discuss the customer focus measures developed for this plant. In chapter 5 we discuss the operational measures developed, and in chapters 6 and 7 some of the local indicators for the same plant.

Prior to designing and using the In-Sync set of measures, the situation of this plant with respect to customer satisfaction was fairly typical. Plant personnel acknowledged the need for satisfied customers, and the new mission statement clearly listed customer focus in its opening line. However, the plant could not say with certainty what the level of customer satisfaction was. It did not track shipments for on-time performance. Weight was tracked, since this information was needed for billing (internal, though critical) purposes. The plant manager knew that delivery performance needed improvement — significantly and quickly. He heard this message from customers louder and clearer each day.

Lead time measures were also non-existent. The only real customer measure was a measure of quality — namely, customer returns for incorrect chemistry or mechanical properties. It is interesting to note that this was used primarily as an expense or cost issue and not as a customer satisfaction issue.

It was ascertained through a quick customer survey that the important issues were on-time deliveries and responsiveness (as measured by lead time). It was also established that customers were, in fact, actively seeking suppliers with on-time deliveries of at least 95 percent and with delivery lead times of 10 days. It was abundantly clear what the customer satisfaction measures needed to be for this plant.

The critical customer performance items were on-time deliveries, order lead time and quality. Figure 4-6 shows the first section of the monthly In-Sync set for this plant dealing with customer satisfaction. Customer measures were reviewed on a weekly basis. Monthly averages were developed for use in monthly In-Sync reports.

Figure 4-6

In-Sync Performance Report

In-Sync Performance Report - Plant Level						
I. Customer Satisfaction	**Jan**	**Feb**	**Mar**	**Apr**	**May**	**Jun**
On-Time Deliveries						
Orders Due	149	163	210	186	118	164
Orders Shipped	125	144	200	173	114	160
Percent on-time	84%	88%	95%	93%	94%	98%
Returns						
Number	1	0	1	2	0	2
Dollar Values (% of Sales)	0.70%	0.00%	0.22%	0.92%	0.00%	0.40%
Lead Time						
Date ordered to date due	17	15	16	12	12	14
Production cycle time	10	10	11	9	7	5

On-time deliveries are defined on a line-item basis. In this case, the customers order each product as a separate order. An order is considered on time if it is shipped on the date specified or the previous day. The report lists the number of orders that fell due during the course of the week, the number that were shipped within the tolerance window and the percent of orders that were "on-time."

Lead time was measured in the following manner. The calculation of date ordered to date due, is simply the number of days the customers were actually allowing the plant to produce and ship the product. This was compared with the demonstrated capability of the plant.

Quality is measured by returns. In this case, the customers return any product that fails to meet specifications. They do not have the option to repair the product or to use the "out-of-spec" product. Hence, returns is a full measure of defective products that were shipped. In the In-Sync report shown in Figure 4-6, returns are measured both by the number of orders that were returned and the dollar value of the returns (measured as a percent of weekly/monthly sales).

The elements that are critical to the customer must be constantly monitored. Weekly evaluation of performance is almost a necessity today. Even if financial performance can only be obtained and reviewed monthly due to financial system limitations, customer satisfaction must be reviewed as frequently as possible. They must also be measured against each product's individual lead time, not for the product line as a whole. In the In-Sync set of measures, customer focus measures are reviewed first and most frequently.

In addition to making sure customers are satisfied with performance today, one must keep an eye on the competition. The fact that customers are happy today will not guarantee that they will be happy tomorrow. The experiences of the U.S. auto industry provides a good example. When the market share of domestic auto manufacturers eroded in the 1970s, it was not because there was a degradation in their own performance. It was because the Japanese small cars were more suited to the times, and the Japanese had surpassed the U.S. manufacturers in quality.

Benchmarking activities like the one described in this chapter should be periodically undertaken to keep abreast of competitors. The nature of the industry determines how frequently this should be done. In the aerospace industry annual reviews of competitive performance may be adequate. In high-tech consumer products evaluations may have to be done monthly.

CHAPTER 5

MEASURES OF OPERATIONAL PERFORMANCE

Business owners and senior executives must look at a minimum of three financial measures to know if their company is making money. These measures are net profit (NP), return on assets (ROA) and cash flow (CF). They must look at the trends relative to these three measures to see if the company's financial performance is improving over time.

In most companies it is difficult to link net profit, return on assets, and cash flow for the company as a whole to the day-to-day activities of the manufacturing operation. Because of this, it is not easy for plant, production and engineering management to understand how the actions they take will actually improve or hurt the company's income statement and balance sheet.

For instance, a shop supervisor assigns a specific job to a specific work center. How does that influence the company's goal of making money? The supervisor works to eliminate a quality problem, or reduce the work force in a given area. How do these actions affect the profits of the entire company?

In the past, manufacturing has been measured on purely local measures — labor efficiency and resource utilization. It has been taken on faith that these standard cost measures translate into global corporate performance. As highlighted in chapter 2, this assumption is not valid. The owner of a small manufacturing company does not depend on such standard cost measures to help him determine whether or not he is making money. He can see the flow of real money — both in sold products (or money received) and expenses (money paid out). The measures we seek to establish try to make everyone's perspective similar to that of an owner.

OPERATIONAL MEASURES DEFINED

To evaluate manufacturing actions, we propose the use of the three **operational** and **global measures** that are specific to manufacturing businesses:

Throughput (T)
Inventory (I)
Operating Expense (OE)

Figure 5-1 shows a schematic of the financial components of the manufacturing system and where T, I, and OE fit into the flow of money. Essentially, there are three basic activities a manufacturing business undertakes:

- The purchase of raw materials and component parts
- The conversion of purchased material into finished products
- The sale of manufactured (fabricated and/or assembled) product

The operational measures of Throughput, Inventory, and Operating Expense relate to these primary activities.

Figure 5-1

The relationship between T, I, and OE, and the flow of money into and out of a business.

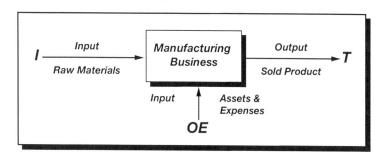

1. **Throughput is money generated through sales, not through production.**

    T = sales - purchased material cost

    The simple change in measuring output at time of sale and not at time of production represents the reality of the shift from a sellers' market to a buyers' market. In a sellers' market it was a safe assumption that everything produced would be sold and sold relatively soon. In a buyers' market this is not the case. As any owner of a manufacturing company knows, a profit is made only when an item is sold, not when it is produced for finished goods inventory. In order to link manufacturing performance measures to real profit, one needs to measure sales rather than production.

    Another key point about this definition that needs emphasis is that it measures output and not activity. Throughput measures output in dollars. It does not measure activity in hours, units, tons, etc. Activity that does not contribute to sales (to the conversion of material into products sold) is wasted. Throughput as defined above shifts the point where manufacturing credits are given — at the point of sale and not at the point of activity — and it shifts the unit of measure — from hours, units, tons, etc., to dollars.

Finally, credit is given only to the value added contribution (as the market sees it), by treating material cost as a pass-through item.

2. **Inventory is the amount of money tied up in materials that the company intends to sell.**

   I = Purchased material value of Raw Material, In-process and Finished Goods Inventories.

Again, this definition differs from the traditional definition of inventory in a number of subtle but important ways. First, it includes only material that the manufacturing company intends to sell. In a typical machine shop, this means that the raw forging being machined is included in the inventory. The cutting tool and the lubricating fluid are not counted in inventory (since the company does not intend to transform these materials and sell them to make money). The rate of conversion of this inventory into throughput represents the ability of the company to respond to changing requirements from the marketplace. Remember, *all* inventories must be reported for balance sheet purposes.

Second, this definition of inventory does not add value as the material is processed. The traditional concept is that inventory absorbs labor and overhead as the material is processed. Under the traditional notion, the inventory value of a raw forging would increase as it goes through the various processing steps. Traditionally, if raw material is valued at $100, then after the first operation the same material could be valued at $110, and when delivered as a finished part to the storeroom it may be valued at $175. In our definition, the inventory value of the part remains at $100, regardless of its stage of production.

The assumption that the "value" of in-process material increases as operations are performed is highly misleading. In reality, not only has no "value" been created, but actual damage has been done. In most manufacturing operations material loses flexibility as it is processed.

A common raw forging may be used in the production of multiple end products. By making the wrong choice of product to machine, not only is no value (or throughput) created, but material is consumed and will have to be replaced when the order for a different product is received. To avoid these sorts of distortions, the value of the inventory is always taken as the original value of the material. The labor and other expenses are accounted for in the next category — operating expense.

3. **Operating expense is money spent to convert Inventory into Throughput.**

   OE = actual spending to turn (I) into (T).

Operating Expense includes all of the money spent by the system with the single exception of inventory purchases. Again, there are a few critical differences with the traditional concept of the cost of operations.

First, no fundamental distinction between direct labor and indirect labor is made in this definition — both should assist in the conversion of inventory into throughput, or in the flow of product to customers. All personnel-related expenses are included in operating expense.

Second, operating expense for the most part includes actual expenses. It counts real money or checks written as opposed to elements such as variances. Under the old system, if an operator is producing product at a faster rate than the engineering standard for the operation, he will be generating a positive variance and the cost of operations will be lowered, even if there is no demand for the product! Under our new definitions, the same situation results in: no change in throughput, an increase in inventory and no change in operating expense (since the operator's wages are unchanged). The standard cost system views labor costs as infinitely variable, while in the In-Sync set, labor costs are viewed as fixed in the short-term.

As shown in Figure 5-1, the material flowing through a manufacturing operation is considered as a pass-through element. It is included in inventory and not in operating expense.

T, I, OE - A SIMPLE EXAMPLE

To illustrate the methodology for computing T, I and OE, consider a small wood shop that makes desks and tables.

To find the throughput, we need to look at the various products sold by this shop and the value of the material in these products. In effect the throughput contribution of each unit sold is found and added to find the total throughput.

To find the contribution to throughput from a desk that sold for $400, one also needs to know the cost of all the material used in the manufacture of the desk. Let's say the cost of the wood, veneer, hardware, etc., used in the desk totals $100. The contribution of this desk to throughput is $300:

T = Sales - Material cost = $400 - $100 = $300

In this way, we calculate the throughput for every product sold. The total throughput for any specific period is obtained by adding the contribution of all the units sold in that period. If this shop sells, in a given month, a total of 50 units ranging in price from $250 to $800, then we obtain the total throughput by adding the contribution from each of the 50 units. The throughput for this month may thus total $15,000.

To find the inventory in the system, one needs to find the purchase value of all the production material currently in the shop. This includes all the wood material in various forms such as chip cores, veneer, cut and raw lumber; it also includes all of the material that is in process and in storerooms, as well as hardware such as drawer hangers, knobs, and hinges. Note again that in this definition of inventory, one values the material at the price paid for it. The value of all of this inventory may, for example, be $32,000. This inventory does not include production tools such as saws, drill and router bits, sanders, etc. Nor does this inventory include other supplies such as coffee cups, paper, etc.

Operating expense includes all of the costs incurred in running the shop and may be displayed as follows:

MONTHLY OPERATING EXPENSES

Category	Amount
Salaries, insurance and payroll taxes	$10,000
Rent and utilities	$750
Supplies (glue, finishing chemicals, etc.)	$200
Payment on equipment purchases	$1800
Inventory carrying costs	$400
Other miscellaneous items	$300
Total Operating Expenses	$13,450

We thus end up with the following values for T, I, and OE:

T = $15,000   I = $32,000   OE = $13,450

T, I, OE AND THE BOTTOM LINE

It is intuitively clear that to make money a manufacturing business must generate more sales, spend less money on conversion of raw material into finished product, and have less money tied up in inventory. To put it simply, a manufacturing company should be trying to accomplish the following:

Throughput should be going up, Inventory should be going down, and Operating Expense should be going down, all at the same time.

To see the relationship between changes in T, I, and OE and the financial performance of the company, we can use the simple wood shop above and evaluate the changes in net profit. (In this example, the net profit is equal to throughput minus operating expenses [$15,000 - $13,450 = $1,550]).

a. Consider an increase in throughput of 10 percent, with inventory and operating expense staying the same. By the definition of T, this would result in an increase in revenues of 10 percent, or $1,500 per month. The cost of the additional material to make the extra units has already been subtracted out. If the additional units were produced by the same work force, which may be possible if they are not bottlenecks, then OE does not change. Hence, all of the extra throughput is profit. In this case, net profit goes up by $1500 per month — from $1,550 to $3,050 — an increase of 96 percent.

b. Consider a reduction in inventory of 10 percent. Since inventory value was $32,000, this means a reduction of $3200. Inventory, as we have defined it, will affect profitability through a reduction in operating expenses. This is because with less money tied up in inventory, there will be less carrying costs. If the carrying costs are 25 percent, then an inventory reduction of $3,200 will result in savings of $800 annually. The profit would clearly go up by this amount per year. The additional profit of $800 represents an increase of 4.3 percent.

c. Consider a reduction in operating expense of 10 percent. The old operating expense was $13,450 per month. A 10 percent reduction amounts to a reduction in expense of $1345 each month. This means that the new monthly expense would be $12,105. With the sales level staying the same, profit would increase by $1345 per month, an increase of 87 percent.

Figure 5-2

Positive performance on the operational measures will improve the financial performance.

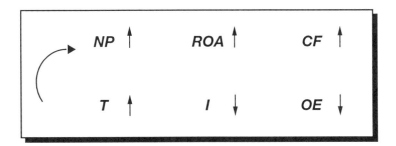

Figure 5-2 shows the relationship between the positive trend in T, I, and OE and the financial objectives. See *Synchronous Manufacturing: Principles For World-Class Excellence* by Umble and Srikanth[1] (pp. 32-34) for a numerical example that relates T, I, and OE to all three financial measures of NP, ROA, and CF.

It is also implied by the symbolic relationship shown in Figure 5-2 that from the numeric values (and changes to) T, I, and OE, the impact on the financial measures of NP, ROA, and CF can be calculated. It should again be emphasized that the operational measures are not replacements for the financial measures. They are the intermediate measures that are more useful in manufacturing environments to assist managers in making more effective decisions.

T, I, AND OE AS DECISION MAKING TOOLS

We are proposing very simply that manufacturing actions and decisions be related first to changes in T, I, and OE. These changes in T, I, and OE can then be used to evaluate changes in the financial measures of NP, ROA, and CF. The operational measures T, I, and OE provide the bridge between manufacturing activities and the financial measures.

This appears to be a simple change in procedure. But it represents a significant change in thought patterns and behavior, both on the factory floor and in the executive offices. It shifts attention from local optimization to global optimization. It changes the focus from local efficiencies and local costs to global impact on the total business.

To illustrate the difference between the traditional view and the synchronous view, consider the operating costs usually assigned to various pieces of equipment. The hourly cost assigned to a work center in a straightforward application of the standard cost system is based on the labor grade assigned to the work center. At the other extreme, an activity-based cost system (ABC) identifies all of the resources (be they in production, support, engineering, etc.) and assigns a rate based on the total value of consumption of that resource. If, for example, there are two pieces of equipment — VTL1 and VMC2 — both of which have the same labor grade and require similar support services, then the cost to operate either work center would be the same in both the standard cost system and the ABC system. There would be very little difference between how these two machines would be treated.

But the impact of the two machines on the total system revenues and costs could be very different. This difference is clearly highlighted when one of the machines is a bottleneck and the other is not. Assume VMC2 is a bottleneck and VTL1 is a non-bottleneck. If VMC2 is disrupted for one hour, the total system throughput will be lost for one hour. This is because the total system output is constrained or limited by the capacity of the bottleneck, VMC2. In the case of a business that has annual sales of $10 million (weekly sales = $200,000), the hourly rate of throughput is $1190 (assuming 168 hours per week). The impact of this disruption would be lost revenues of $1190.

The impact of disrupting VTL1 for one hour is minimal. It is a non-bottleneck, and hence has some level of excess capacity. VTL1 can thus recover from the disruption, with no impact on the total system. Even if this resulted in some overtime, the dollar impact remains orders of magnitude smaller than the impact of an hour lost at VMC2.

This clear difference between the two resources ($1,190 per hour at VMC2 and almost zero at VTL1) has an impact on a host of decisions — value of off-loading work from VMC2, cost of carrying back-up tooling, cost of preventive maintenance, etc. The view, whether through the standard cost system or the ABC system, does not differentiate between VTL1 and VMC2 and would treat them in exactly the same way. Meanwhile, the synchronous view would appropriately differentiate between one piece of equipment which has some excess capacity from another piece of equipment whose capacity is limiting the performance of the entire business.

THE RATIOS T/I AND T/OE

In evaluating performance, the ratios T/I and T/OE are more useful than the numerical values of T, I, and OE themselves. Good performance — T increasing while I and OE are decreasing — can be stated in terms of the ratios T/I increasing and T/OE increasing simultaneously. Also, the use of the ratios forces the organization to consider all the measures simultaneously.

The **ratio T/I** measures the effectiveness with which inventory, or material investments, is converted into throughput. It is a measure of the velocity of material flow through the operation. The higher the value of this ratio, the faster the flow of product, which in turn implies faster responsiveness, shorter production lead times and lower inventories.

The ratio T/I is not linear in its behavior with changing market conditions. As sales increase, T/I may increase at first, but as one begins to exhaust the production capacity, inventory will build up and T/I will decline.

Consider the wood shop discussed earlier. What is the impact on the ratio T/I if they sell one more desk per month? The answer to this simple question depends on how loaded the shop is at this point in time. If plenty of capacity is available then the production of this additional desk will have minimal impact on inventory. Hence, the ratio T/I will improve.

On the other hand, if the shop is near its capacity limit, then the impact of this additional unit is significant. The time to produce the additional unit will be at the expense of the reactive capacity that was available before. It will take longer for the shop to recover from day-to-day disruptions, and this means that lead times, and hence inventory, will increase significantly. In this case, it is possible that the ratio T/I will actually decrease.

The **ratio T/OE** can be viewed as a measure of total productivity. It represents the amount of money earned for each dollar expended. In the simple case of steady-state market conditions (T remaining fixed), it is expected that good management will find ways to improve operations through process improvements, inventory reductions, and the like, so that the ratio T/OE will increase from year to year.

The real objective is to translate these improvements into market opportunities and generate more sales, thus driving T up. How T/OE behaves as market conditions change — and hence how T changes — will vary from business to business and from plant to plant. This is because both T and OE come in discrete elements without a simple link between one unit of T and one unit of OE.

Returning to the wood shop example, if the company sells one less desk, clearly throughput is reduced. But there is no one element of expense (personnel, utilities, equipment, etc.) similarly reduced. Every percent reduction in sales cannot be matched by a percent reduction in OE.

Conversely, if the shop sells one more desk it may not be necessary to hire any new workers; it may not even be necessary to add any overtime. The people in the shop may be capable of producing the one additional unit. Thus, every percent increase in sales does not necessarily require a percent increase in operating expenses.

One should not expect the T/OE ratio to remain constant as sales level changes. A key piece of information for every manager to know is the expected behavior of the T/OE ratio with small volume changes, given the current expense profile. It is also important to understand how the behavior will change when the OE profile changes, such as with the purchase of new equipment (to add capacity or replace labor). In fact, the best time to do this analysis is before the changes are made. Most managers do some of this analysis today, but it is done intuitively, locally and on gut feel. Efficiency and unit cost data, which form the basis of the current formal system at most companies, do not provide much help.

The behavior of the ratios T/I and T/OE are not mutually exclusive. It is possible to make tradeoffs, decreasing one ratio to improve the other. A small addition to capacity, which might reduce T/OE, might enable significant improvements in T/I. The next section discusses these issues further. More important in the current competitive market situation is that the behavior of the ratios is affected by changes in the nature of the throughput. By this we mean that changes in volatility of the demand,

Figure 5-3

Operational Measures

Operational Measures						
	Jan	**Feb**	**Mar**	**Apr**	**May**	**Jun**
Throughput						
Monthly Figure	152	224	288	194	299	178
Rolling Average	181	182	192	191	198	196
Inventory						
At Month End	414	410	395	405	387	380
Rolling Average	449	445	432	426	419	414
Operating Expenses						
Monthly Figure	174	169	167	165	156	156
Rolling Average	170	170	170	169	168	167
T/I Ratio (Annualized)						
At Month End	4.4	6.6	8.7	5.7	9.3	5.6
Rolling Average	4.8	4.9	5.3	5.4	5.7	5.7
T/OE Ratio						
Monthly Figure	0.9	1.3	1.7	1.2	1.9	1.1
Rolling Average	1.1	1.1	1.1	1.1	1.2	1.2

the lead times customers are willing to accept, the stringency with which delivery dates are to be met, etc., all influence the value of the ratios T/I and T/OE.

Figure 5-4

a) Throughput ($000)

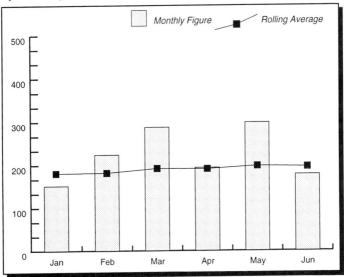

b) Inventory ($000)

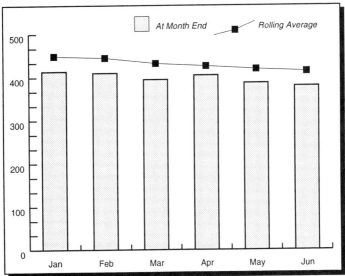

Figure 5-4

c) Operating Expenses ($000)

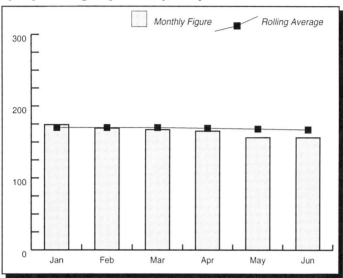

d) T/I Ratio (Annualized)

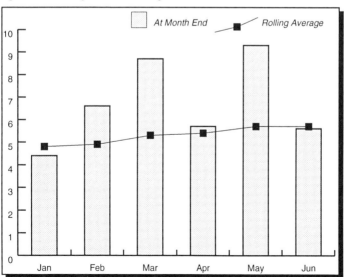

Figure 5-4

e) T/OE Ratio

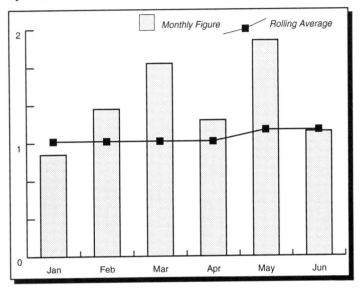

In trying to use the numerical values of T, I, and OE, or the T/I and T/OE ratios, the snapshot or "instantaneous" values may show significant fluctuations. Daily or weekly production volumes fluctuate due to variability in the internal system, as well as variability from external sources — variability in the rate of production and the rate of sales and variability in the mix of products being sold. Therefore, rolling averages could be used to dampen the statistical fluctuations and show trends more effectively. Figures 5-3 and 5-4 show the numerical values and the graphic representation of the operational measures — the actual values as well as the rolling averages.

To summarize, the benefits of using the synchronous measures of T, I, and OE for evaluating operational performance are:

1. They link manufacturing decisions to sales. Since customers must be won and retained, this is a necessary pre-condition for effective decision making. These measures clearly promote the "manufacturing is a sales driver" philosophy.

2. They drive speed and flexibility. Note that in this system, inventory occupies a more important role than cost. This is because of the clear link between inventory and the critical competitive elements of speed, flexibility, and quality. Actions that reduce inventory are actions that improve competitive performance.

3. These measures encompass all the spending under a manager's control. They balance cost reduction with improvements in the competitive elements. Expenses, and hence costs, are not ignored, but are placed in the proper perspective. Actions that result in cost reduction should meet two criteria:

    (i) They should result in real money being saved and not just "calculated" savings.
    (ii) They should not adversely affect customer satisfaction or competitive performance.

4. They help maintain a global orientation and discourage local optimization, since they help evaluate global impact rather than just local effects of decisions.

5. These measures clearly link decisions and actions to making money. The language of T, I, and OE is real money — money earned and money spent. There are no variances or other such accounting nuances. This should enable people to relate to their unit as a business with the clear objective of making money.

RESETTING OPERATING BUDGETS - THE CRUCIAL LINK

It is not enough to simply measure and post T, I, and OE values instead of labor hour and efficiency measures. The new measures must be the basis for the decision making process that drives the organization. This will not be the case unless budgets and performance targets are also established using the new measures.

Budgets play an extremely critical role in every organization. It is the primary control or review tool used by most senior managers. In addition, performance relative to budgets is often a key determinant of a manager's performance or incentive compensation. Few managers can afford to overlook budgetary indicators.

The solution is to restate the budgets in terms of the new measures. The traditional approach to the establishment and use of budgets has two major drawbacks:

1. It suffers from the internal focus and excessive emphasis on direct labor that characterizes the traditional accounting system.

2. In practice, budgets tend to be too detailed and attempt to control expenses at a very local level. They tend to micro manage the operation.

The way the traditional system establishes targets and tries to control performance ultimately encourages local optimization with particular emphasis on direct labor. Thus, budgets under the traditional system have the wrong emphasis, serve as a micro-management tool, and encourage local optimization.

A clear example from real life illustrates the problem very well. At one plant, the local managers had very successfully implemented synchronous management concepts to the management of work flow throughout the manufacturing operation. They had made major reductions in inventory on the floor, as well as in finished goods inventory. Customer overdues, the major market complaint, had been almost eliminated. But inventory of chemicals and other materials used by this plant had increased. This was due to the simple fact that the plant could not shut off the supply of raw material as fast as they had shut off production, in order to drain the inventory and focus on producing the right product at the right time. The result was a variance in the line item labeled "supply inventory."

The head office in New York promptly inquired about this variance as well as the under absorption. Even when told about the synchronous activities that had been initiated and the positive results in customer service and finished goods inventory that had been achieved, the head office was not impressed. The plant manager was told to "do whatever is necessary to correct the variances," even if that meant making product that could not be sold.

Clearly, if the company had been tracking In-Sync measures, they would not have been concerned about the situation in the plant. In fact, both customer measures and the ratios T/I and T/OE showed significant improvement. This example also highlights the fact that manufacturing is an interdependent activity, and local measures and controls should be used with great care.

While the above example illustrates an extreme case, budgets and the many different items that make up the budget exert a strong influence on what line managers do. It is imperative that budgets be redone using the new measures.

We are not talking here of making sure that the graphs and charts in the cafeteria are all done in the language of the new measures. We are talking about the formal document that will be used when the group vice-president visits the local plant. It is this document and the language and items that make up this discussion that really determine what the plant manager, and hence the plant, will actually do.

In a highly competitive marketplace demand tends to be volatile. Hence, fixed budgets based on spending alone do not have much relevance. Instead, budgets should be established for the ratios T/I and T/OE. Along with the understanding of how these ratios should behave with changes in business volume, monitoring the ratios will enable senior management to assess the performance of line managers.

EXAMPLE OF OPERATIONAL MEASURES AT THE PLANT LEVEL

The operational measures for the primary metal manufacturer, discussed at the end of chapter 3, make up section II of the In-Sync report, shown again in Figure 5-5. At the plant level, operational performance is measured by throughput and the ratios T/I and T/OE. These measures are computed and reviewed on a monthly basis.

In this case, throughput is based on the sales value (minus material cost) of the products shipped during the month. In the report, "dollars due" is the potential throughput that could have been realized if all products due in a given month were shipped that month. "Dollars shipped" is the sales value (minus material cost) of products actually shipped minus any returns from, or credits to, customers. The difference indicates to all employees of the plant the opportunity that was lost or, at least, delayed.

Figure 5-5
In-Sync Performance Report

In-Sync Performance Report - Plant Level						
I. Customer Satisfaction	**Jan**	**Feb**	**Mar**	**Apr**	**May**	**Jun**
On-Time Deliveries						
Orders Due	149	163	210	186	118	164
Orders Shipped	125	144	200	173	114	160
Percent on-time	84%	88%	95%	93%	94%	98%
Returns						
Number	1	0	1	2	0	2
Dollar Values	0.70%	0.00%	0.22%	0.92%	0.00%	0.40%
(% of Sales)						
Lead Time						
Date ordered to date due	17	15	16	12	12	14
Production cycle time	10	10	11	9	7	5
II. Operational Performance	**Jan**	**Feb**	**Mar**	**Apr**	**May**	**Jun**
Throughput						
Dollars Due	7,136	7,424	6,892	6,372	5,024	5,620
Dollars Shipped	5,240	6,976	6,168	6,272	4,852	5,592
T/I						
Turns (Annualized)	10.0	14.3	13.9	15.2	13.2	16.1
T/OE	1.25	1.37	1.27	1.29	1.25	1.36

Inventory and operating expense are measured through the ratios T/I and T/OE. Inventory, in this case, includes in-process and finished goods inventories. These are valued at the purchase price of the raw materials. The raw material inventory is not included since some of the inventory is on consignment, and some is owned by the customers, and some is shared with sister plants producing different materials. For the purchasing group and the division, the inventory number would certainly include all of this material.

Operating expenses include all of the expenses incurred at the plant for personnel, equipment, production supplies, and buildings. Equipment costs are included through depreciation charges. Divisional charges are excluded.

The In-Sync report uses the ratios T/I and T/OE rather than the absolute numbers of inventory and operating expense. The ratios were chosen since the latter would mean little to line employees. Both inventory and a significant portion of expenses fluctuate with sales/production volume. Without comparison to the output level, no judgment can be made about fluctuations in I and OE. The added advantage is that the level of inventory and the level of plant spending are compared to actual sales (or business) activity and not to budget numbers because budgets are set six to twelve months earlier, and the business conditions may have changed significantly.

By measuring operational performance based on the dollar value of orders due and orders shipped in the month, and the ratios T/I and T/OE, the focus of all employees is kept on sales and on the relative levels of inventory and expenses.

CHAPTER 6

CONSTRAINT MEASURES

The customer (or external) measures and the operational performance (or internal) measures give a company their overall score. They tell whether the company is winning or losing and which of the two sides (customer side or internal operational performance) must be improved more urgently than the other. But they fall short of telling why the company is losing and do not help identify specific corrective actions that need to be taken. For this purpose, more local information that can tie the performance of a specific local area or work center to the performance of the organization is needed. This is the purpose of the constraint measures.

As an example of the need for and nature of constraint measures, consider the coach of a football team that just lost a series of games by the average score of 10 to 3. How can the coach identify the specific improvements necessary to improve the team's performance? The overall score does tell the coach which general areas need improvement.

From the scores (average points allowed = 10; average points scored = 3) and even a casual knowledge of the game, we all recognize that the problem with this team is that it did not score enough points. A good coach would know from looking at league scores that the league average for points scored is 20. The defense has held the opposition to half the league average, while the offense has scored well below the average. The coach may even know that against a specific opponent who generally allows 14 points per game, his team only scored 6 points. All of this information enables the coach to quickly identify that the problem is with the offense and not with the defense. Note, however, that beyond providing that general guideline the team score is not of much use in helping the coach identify on which areas the team needs to work and certainly provides little help to individual players.

In the case of football teams, the information needed to identify specific improvements comes from a host of detailed measures and statistics that are compiled and maintained for each play in each game. These include yards per carry, yards passing, percent completions, yards rushing, first downs, etc. These local indicators help coaches identify which areas of their team's play need improvement and also help individual players identify what they need to do better in order for the overall team performance to improve.

The information necessary for significant and steady improvement is two-fold. First, coaches (business managers) need a process and the associated information to assist them in identifying the weakest area — the constraint. This may, for example, be the left side of the offensive line. The game plan can then be constructed to minimize the impact of this weakness and to begin the process of remedying this weakness. The measures that help monitor and track performance of the constraint are called constraint measures. This chapter will deal with constraint measures.

Second, each player needs to be able to identify how he can help improve the team performance. This applies whether we are talking about an offensive or defensive player. Every player can improve, even the best player on the team. The growth and improvement of every player should be encouraged. Coaches must work with individual players to ensure that these improvements are what the team needs. In other words, each player must be encouraged to improve the aspect of his game that will have the most positive impact on the team. The measures that help the players focus on what to improve are called activity-focusing measures, and are discussed in chapter 7.

CONSTRAINTS

In the context of a manufacturing organization, constraints are identified by answering the key question:

What specific area, aspect or process limits the business' performance from a customer, competitive or profit point of view?

The concept of constraints helps focus managerial activities for maximum leverage. By definition, a constraint is that aspect of an operation that limits the performance of the entire organization. Constraints thus have the maximum impact on the organization's ultimate (financial) performance. Everyone's eyes should be on the constraint. In the case of the football team discussed earlier, the left side of the offensive line was the constraint area. A systematic way is needed to go from the team performance (overall business issue) to the specific key problem with the left side of the offensive line (constraint). This is provided by the constraint identification methodology.

The identification of constraints requires a solid understanding of the interdependencies of the business. It is not an exaggeration to say that no management task is more important than to ensure that the organization has a sound understanding of these interdependencies. Management should continuously challenge the soundness of the reasoning used in identifying constraints. The clearest indication that the constraint has been properly identified is that improvement in the local indicators for this area will result in improved global measures. If this does not happen, then the constraint has been misidentified!

The methodology of identifying the most critical step, or the **Constraint Identification Methodology** as it is called in synchronous management, can not be done using only global measures or the information needed to calculate them. For example, by examining the global measure, one can determine not only the number of late orders, but also the extent to which the orders are late. However, it can not be determined, from the global measure, the cause of a specific late order. To fix the problem the cause needs to be identified. For this, a different set of information is needed.

Identifying constraints in a manufacturing operation is not a trivial exercise for two major reasons:

1. Manufacturing businesses are composed of highly interdependent and complex activities.

2. The impact of the same identical action, at different points or areas of the business, can be very different.

These key points are summarized in the synchronous principle that the sum of local optimums may not equal the global optimum. The book *Synchronous Manufacturing: Principles For World-Class Excellence*[1] discusses how capacity constraints (or bottlenecks) can be identified.

CONSTRAINT MEASURES

There are two aspects to constraints: their position in the flow and the characteristics identifying them as constraints. Once the location and nature of the constraint have been identified, the measures to monitor performance of the constraint can be developed. These are the **constraint measures.**

For example, if material availability is a constraint, then the amount of material received from the supplier and the amount of material scrapped, or otherwise misallocated in the production process, would be constraint measures.

Constraint measures are more important than all the other step-specific and local measures that will continue to be collected, reviewed and utilized at the local levels. Constraint measures are key to improving the overall score. As a result, they are part of the In-Sync set at the business level and should be reviewed by senior management regularly.

Constraint measures will replace budgetary variance items. Variances, particularly as calculated by the standard cost system, have little bearing on the overall company performance. Constraint measures, by definition, are measures of those items with the most impact on the overall company performance. By reviewing the global performance measures and the constraint measures, management will be reviewing both the overall score and the measures for the areas that must be improved for performance of the entire unit to improve.

Before proceeding with a process for developing constraint measures, let us look at a simple example that illustrates the concept.

CONSTRAINT MEASURES - A SIMPLE EXAMPLE

Consider the small wood shop discussed in earlier chapters. The shop is too small to have meaningful sub-units. Measurements go from the business level to the individual activity level. Comparison of performance to targets might reveal that the most significant gap to address is on-time performance.

Working back from the shipping department might reveal a capacity bottleneck at the cabinet maker. This is confirmed as the key constraint to delivery performance by the synchronous constraint identification methodology. The cabinet maker will have to be productively utilized (as defined in synchronous manufacturing) all of his available time. Time lost at the cabinet maker is sales lost for the entire business. Hence, **the utilization of the cabinet maker becomes the constraint measure.** In addition to the global measures defined in chapters 4 and 5, such as delivery performance, quality, throughput, inventory, and operating expense, the utilization of the cabinet maker needs to be monitored. The global measures and the constraint measures complete the structured set.

The In-Sync set for the senior manager of the wood shop would be :

Customer performance measure =
    On-time deliveries, returns, complaints, promised lead times.
Operational Measures =
    Throughput, Inventory, Operating Expenses.
Constraint measure = Utilization of cabinet maker.

The measures to assist other areas of the shop in making improvements (in finishing, for example) will be discussed in chapter 7.

SYSTEMATIC APPROACH
TO DEVELOPING CONSTRAINT MEASURES

Returning to the example of the football team, a two-step process was needed to identify the critical weakness or constraint. The first step was to identify that the offense was the weakness, and this was done using global measures. Then the left side of the line was identified as the weakest area and this was done using local measures, such as yards per carry, etc. However, manufacturing businesses are more complex than football teams.

Figure 6-1
Systematic process for developing constraint measures.

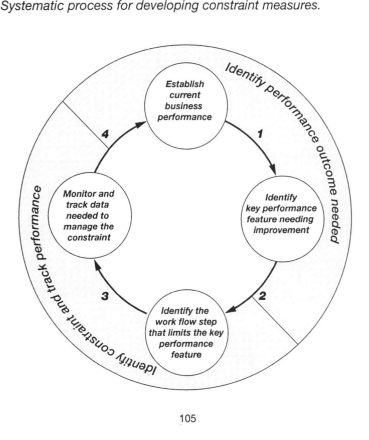

To make the process of developing constraint measures simple, we have broken down the systematic process into four steps as shown in Figure 6-1. The first two steps get us to identifying which performance outcome needs to be improved. The third and fourth steps help identify and track constraints.

Step 1: Establish current performance of the business.

>   This is the answer to the question: *How is the company doing?* or, *What is the performance to customers and to owners?* For the business as a whole, this is provided by the global measures discussed in chapters 4 and 5. It basically relates to how well the business is meeting expectations from customers and owners.

Step 2: Identify the key performance feature needing improvement.

>   This is the answer to: *What aspect of performance needs to improve first?* Remember that in trying to answer this question, one must start with the external view — by asking what needs to be done to attract new customers and increase sales. If all customers are reasonably happy but the company is operating at a loss, then one needs to focus on internal operational measures. As constraints are systematically identified and resolved, it is reasonable to expect that the focus will shift back and forth between external and internal performance issues.

>   The process for finding the key performance factor is straightforward. Using customer surveys, industry data, competitive benchmarking and so on, one can establish the performance levels required.

Comparison of actual performance to targets will help identify the performance features with the most serious gaps. External measures will carry a heavier weight factor in highly competitive markets.

Step 3: **Identify the specific step in the work flow that is the limiting factor for these key performance features.**

This step answers the question: *What is the constraint?* or, *What is the root cause of performance shortfalls or opportunities?* This is essentially the identification of the system constraint. A "step in the flow of work" is not restricted to a production or manufacturing step. It can be an activity or an entire business process in the office. For example, the problem may not be a specific machine or work center; it could be the procurement process.

Step 4: **Monitor and regularly track the data needed to manage the constraint.**

This provides the answer to: *What are the constraint measures?* As discussed before, there are two aspects to constraints — where they are in the flow, and what feature makes them a constraint. In the simplest case, a work center (machine) can be a capacity constraint (bottleneck) because of the total work it is required to perform. Or it can be a capacity constraint because of serious maintenance problems reducing its available capacity.

This set of information finally gets us to the **constraint measures.** These are the constraint measures for the entire business and belong in the In-Sync set at the business level.

Let's look at some examples of constraint measures.

Example 1

Consider the case of a furniture manufacturer where on-time delivery and inventory are the key performance features needing improvement. The constraint identification methodology leads to the key issues affecting on-time delivery. They are the availability of component parts at final assembly and demand surges causing overloads at the assembly operation.

Constraint measures should then be designed to indicate the status of component availability. The status of buffer inventories (measured by "stock outs" or a buffer less than 50 percent full) serves this purpose. To identify the magnitude of demand surges, the rate of incoming orders (measured against assembly capacity) serves as an example of a constraint measure.

Example 2

Consider the case of a job shop (with a hundred work centers and several hundred work orders on the floor) where on-time delivery is the key performance feature needing improvement. The constraint identification methodology leads management to the issue of assignment of priorities in the shop as the constraint.

In this case, the business process needing improvement is schedule discipline at each work center. Some products are worked on early, while other jobs are allowed to languish. The problem is misallocation of resource capacity. The constraint measure in this case can be percent of orders completed early (ahead of schedule), since this is a clear indication of capacity misallocation.

Example 3

Consider the case of a machine shop supplying the automotive industry, where the key performance feature needing improvement is to produce sufficient product to satisfy strong market demand. The issue, in terms of the global measures, is to increase Throughput. The constraint identification methodology leads to the availability of a key purchased component. Constraint measures in this case include the number of component units received weekly, and the number of products that were in rework or scrapped (representing misallocation of the constraint — the key purchased component).

As these examples illustrate, the constraint measures can be machine or product specific or may be statistical in nature.

The constraint measures complete the In-Sync set at the business level. This means that senior managers must review these measures on a regular basis. It provides them the information about the score, through the customer and operational measures. It also helps them "keep their finger on the pulse" through the constraint measures. Senior managers are provided the full global picture. They are also provided the details where it counts, namely at the constraint.

Measures to help manage and make improvements are also needed at all of the non-constraint areas of a business. The development of these measures will be discussed in the next chapter.

EXAMPLE OF CONSTRAINT MEASURES
AT THE PLANT LEVEL

Figure 6-2 shows the complete In-Sync set for the primary metal manufacturer used as example in chapters 4 and 5. As discussed in chapter 4, the customer measures of importance in this case are delivery performance, lead time to fulfill the order, and returns. The operational performance, as discussed in chapter 5, is measured by throughput (T) and the ratios T/I and T/OE.

Figure 6-2
In-Sync Performance Report

In-Sync Performance Report - Plant Level						
I. Customer Satisfaction	**Jan**	**Feb**	**Mar**	**Apr**	**May**	**Jun**
On-Time Deliveries						
Orders Due	149	163	210	186	118	164
Orders Shipped	125	144	200	173	114	160
Percent on-time	84%	88%	95%	93%	97%	98%
Returns						
Number	1	0	1	2	0	2
Dollar Values (% of Sales)	0.70%	0.00%	0.22%	0.92%	0.00%	0.40%
Lead Time						
Date ordered to date due	17	15	16	12	12	14
Production cycle time	10	10	11	9	7	5
II. Operational Performance	**Jan**	**Feb**	**Mar**	**Apr**	**May**	**Jun**
Throughput						
Dollars Due	7,136	7,424	6,892	6,372	5,024	5,620
Dollars Shipped	5,240	6,976	6,168	6,272	4,852	5,592
T/I						
Turns (Annualized)	10.0	14.3	13.9	15.2	13.2	16.1
T/OE	1.25	1.37	1.27	1.29	1.25	1.36
III. Constraint Measures	**Jan**	**Feb**	**Mar**	**Apr**	**May**	**Jun**
Final Finishing						
Output to plan	78	69	88	92	95	97
Furnace Yields						
#1 Furnace	83.6	84.0	82.1	82.2	82.7	84.0
#2 Furnace	86.1	87.3	87.5	87.2	86.8	87.2

The business issues for this primary metal producer are to improve the on-time delivery performance and to control expenses. Thus, on-time deliveries and expenses become the key performance features needing improvement.

The constraint to on-time performance was identified as the output of the final machining/finishing operations. This conclusion is bolstered by key observations from the shop floor — the work queue at finishing consistently represents three to five days of work; expediters frequently complain of work held up at finishing; overtime is common.

A work load analysis using projected demand also shows that the finishing department is close to being a capacity constraint. Hence, close attention to the output of this department is required. Output of the finishing department is one of the constraint measures. In this case, the constraint measure is defined as the number of units actually completed as a percent of the plan.

As for expenses, the other key performance feature needing improvement, the major factor is material yield at the two furnaces. Thus, the yield at each furnace becomes one of the constraint measures. The yield is defined as the total value of raw material that goes into the furnace versus the value of good units that are passed on to the finishing operations. The value is computed using the purchase price of the raw materials.

For this primary metals producer, the constraint measures consist of the output of the final finishing department and the yields at the two furnaces.

The complete In-Sync set reviewed monthly by plant management is shown in Figure 6-2. Plant management will see the overall score from the customer satisfaction measures (on-time delivery, returns, and cycle time) and from the operational performance measures (T, T/I, and T/OE). By monitoring the constraint measures (output at finishing and yields at furnaces) management will be monitoring the constraints, the key areas which are currently limiting the performance of the entire plant.

CHAPTER 7

ACTIVITY-OUTCOME AND ACTIVITY-FOCUSING MEASURES

The process of developing the global In-Sync set of measures can be summarized as follows:

1. Define the appropriate set of customer and operational measures that will be used to evaluate the unit's performance. Establish targets for performance and monitor on a regular basis.

2. Optimize opportunity for achieving results by identifying and focusing on constraints. Constraint measures provide business managers with the information to manage constraints. Instead of averaging, accumulating or otherwise summarizing performance of all of the myriad business activities, the synchronous approach identifies the vital activities and collects detailed information necessary to monitor these activities.

Constraints, due to their critical role in determining overall business performance, are singled out, and carefully monitored and controlled. But constraints represent a small percentage of the total resources and activities in any organization. To continue to manage the vast majority of non-constraint activities by "the old numbers" would be to abdicate control of these activities to the old standard cost mindset and measures. We must develop a replacement set of measures for the various sub-units of an organization, such as business units, departments or plants, work centers, and so on. In this chapter the term "local" will be used to refer to any of the business' sub-units.

The local indicators under the traditional cost system are the familiar budget variances. The most prominent local indicator is labor variance. However, performance to the engineered time standard is only one of many elements that go into producing and delivering products and services, so that customers are satisfied and the company is profitable.

In fact, labor variance has no relationship to the external customer-oriented measures. In the traditional direct labor-based cost system, it is assumed that there is a clear connection between labor variances and profits. However, as discussed before, even this connection is greatly exaggerated by the peculiar structure of the cost system.

Most of the latest thinking in the accounting profession reflects the fact that labor costs, and hence labor variances, are but one of many elements that contribute to the expense side of a manufacturing operation. While the evolving theories are free from the labor myopia of the standard cost system, real manufacturing companies continue to be dominated by the standard cost system, and labor variance continues to be the primary local indicator.

The process of developing appropriate local measures starts by understanding the results that are expected to be delivered by that local area. At a local area, the measures that help evaluate performance relative to desired results will be called **activity-outcome measures**. Measures that assist in focusing on the key aspects to ensure performance will be called **activity-focusing measures**.

To illustrate activity-outcome and activity focusing measures, consider a simple example.

EXAMPLE OF ACTIVITY-OUTCOME AND ACTIVITY-FOCUSING MEASURES

Let's return to the wood shop discussed in earlier chapters. We have seen the global measures and the constraint measures. Since the system constraint was the cabinet maker, the outcome of the cabinet maker's activities were discussed under the constraint measures.

In this same shop, what are the appropriate measures for the finishing operator? His task is to complete (i.e. appropriately finish) all the assembled cases given to him. He assists the shop's objectives by rapidly finishing all the cases as required by the customer and without defect. Measures to assist him include the total cases finished in a day, the size of his work queue at the end of the day, the number of finishing mistakes (applying Oak finish when the customer ordered Walnut finish), and reworks due to finishing errors. These are his **activity-outcome measures**.

To focus his activities, the finishing operator must begin by asking how he can help the business improve. On-time delivery has been identified as the most important performance feature needing improvement for this shop. The most significant contribution the finishing operator can make to on-time delivery is to avoid mistakes. The application of the wrong finish causes the most serious rework (complete strip down) and sometimes can not be done at all, causing a loss of throughput.

The **activity-focusing measure** in the case of the finishing operator could be the number of mistakes per 100 cases. The finishing operator's focus should be on minimizing errors by carefully reading the instruction packet, and going in search of the packet when it is misplaced in the cabinet room, instead of applying the "standard finish."

ACTIVITY-OUTCOME MEASURES

The development of activity-outcome measures starts by understanding the desired outcome of the activity in question. It begins by trying to answer the question:

How does this activity help the business satisfy customers and make a profit doing so?

Through this question the focus of the individual employees is moved from their local task to the outcome for the group. It accomplishes at the local/individual level the transition from the internal focus of the old system to the external focus required by the new system. Remember that changing the organizational focus means changing the individual focus and this step begins the process.

The synchronous approach develops the set of measures to assist all levels of the organization in answering the above question from their individual perspective. This approach begins at the business level. Then, through the techniques of synchronous management, one can relate local activities to the performance of the entire business. From this understanding it is possible to develop local measures that are relevant to the organization as a whole. The two aspects that must be kept in mind in developing such activity-outcome measures are:

1. Local activities must be focused on the performance of the total organization. The items measured may relate to individual activities at a local site, but their relevance is determined by their impact on the total organization.

2. Manufacturing organizations are highly interdependent. A solid understanding of these interdependencies is required to establish cause-effect relationships and to relate local activities (or results of local activities) to the organization's performance.

In most organizations, individuals often clearly understand the specific tasks they are required to perform. Most often, they describe themselves in terms of this task. "I am an order-entry clerk, drill-press operator, programmer, etc." It is necessary to enlarge their view to the larger business process in which they are involved. They need to be educated and encouraged to look at themselves as involved in the "order fulfillment process, the manufacturing process, etc." In addition, managers should make them more aware of the results of their activities as measured by their "customers."

For example, an order entry clerk in the order fulfillment process needs to provide operations personnel with certain information. This information should convey customers' needs and desires with regard to product choice, quantity and time of delivery, and price. Because accuracy and timeliness of this information is critical to the entire process, both should be measured and tracked. The percentage of orders with complete information and the average time from receipt of order to entry into the system are examples of activity-outcome measures. The business managers should establish performance and improvement targets for the order entry activity in terms of these measures.

The traditional system of measures with its emphasis on budgetary controls is focused on controlling effort or activity. The In-Sync set measures results and the effort to achieve the global result. The In-Sync set has built into it the opportunity to "empower" individuals or sub-units of the business to organize the activities by focusing on results and not micro-managing the activities. Individuals understand the importance of their activities in the global context. They now take more pride in "being an integral part" of a process than if they focus solely on a task they are required to perform.

DEPARTMENT AND BUSINESS UNIT LEVEL MEASURES

When the business is large (a division of a Fortune 500 company with multiple plants, for instance), it makes sense to look at sub-units that are large and self-contained such that they can be treated as businesses in their own right. "Global" external and operational measures can then be defined for these sub-units. However necessary and meaningful such a sub-unit may be, its relationship to the entire business should not be forgotten. These sub-unit "businesses" are there to serve the larger business, and their global measures can be taken as local measures by the parent business.

For example, a division may include multiple plants that manufacture different components and a plant that assembles these components. Each plant can, and probably should, have an independent set of customer-based measures (on-time delivery, quality, etc.) and operational measures (T/I and T/OE). But each plant should be fully aware of, and feel ownership for, the performance of the division as a whole as well. This is in sharp contrast to traditional measures, which go overboard to separate performance and contribution of sub-units.

The plant itself may be further subdivided into smaller organizational units. If these sub-units are organized along the line of business units or along the line of business processes (as used in current reengineering literature), then it again becomes possible to define "global" external measures for these business units. These global measures (for the business units) are the activity-outcome measures for the plant.

Such "decomposition," from division to plant to business process, allows for consistency of purpose as well as consistency of measures. This is illustrated in Figure 7-1. For each organizational level (division, plant and shop department) the table shows the type of measure that is appropriate for that level. Finally, Figure 7-1 shows examples of the measures appropriate for each organizational level.

Figure 7-1

Examples of types of measures appropriate for various organizational levels.

Organizational Level	Performance Measure	Example of Performance Measure
Corporate or Division	Global In-Sync measures	Delivery, Returns, Price, etc., T, I, OE
Business Unit	In-Sync measures	Delivery, Quality, T, I, OE
Local Activity	Activity-outcome measures	Quantity, Schedule attainment, Inventory, OE

ACTIVITY-FOCUSING MEASURES

Let's return to the football game analogy and look at the defensive unit of the team. Even though it is not the system constraint, the defensive unit can still improve. While being very good, it has relatively strong and weak areas. It makes sense to identify the weakest defensive area and work on this aspect first.

The same approach would apply to any business. Every sub-unit or activity, even those without system constraints, can improve performance relative to most of the measured outcomes. However, some improvements will have a larger impact on the overall business than others.

For each work center the evaluation begins with the following key question:

What specific area, aspect or process within our span of control do we need to improve to achieve the maximum impact on the entire business?

In answering this question, start with the business needs, which are driven by external or customer needs. It is important to ensure that for each individual activity, the performance factor or activity-outcome that has the most significant impact on the total business is clearly understood. The transfer of expectations from the business level to successively deeper levels of the organization is not a trivial task. It is a critical management task to ensure that this transfer of expectations is done properly and is reviewed continuously.

To continue the example of the order entry department, timeliness may be the most important outcome that must be improved to help the entire business. It may currently take five days between the time the company receives a customer order and the time manufacturing receives a production order. To achieve competitive lead time goals, it may be necessary to reduce this time to two days. Order turnaround time is the key activity-outcome that needs to improve.

An activity-focusing measure in this case would be the ratio of process time to the total order turnaround time. The process time is the amount of time during which someone is actually dealing with the order — verifying it, entering the information in the computer, talking to the customer for clarification, and so on. The order turnaround time is the elapsed calendar time between receiving the order and creating a production order. The activity-focusing measure should focus attention on the large percentage of idle time during which there is no activity in processing the order. Examples of things that can be done to reduce the wait time of the order include combining operations to fewer steps (ideally just one), establishing work rules to streamline the flow of paper/information, eliminating redundancy through the use of common data bases or systems, etc.

FOCUSING MEASURES AT DEPARTMENT AND BUSINESS UNIT LEVELS

The constraint measures discussed in chapter 6 provide the focusing measures for the entire business. The process of defining the focusing measures for sub-units is similar to that for the entire business. The process begins by identifying the key performance gaps for the unit (plant or business unit). This involves answering the question: *What improvement in performance at this unit will have the most impact on the performance of the entire business?* Note that the improvement of the unit has meaning only through its impact on the total business. Once the improvements at the unit level are identified, then through the constraint identification methodology one can identify the "local constraint" to improving the business unit. The constraint measures for this local constraint become the focusing measures for this local unit.

The four step process for developing activity-focusing measures is shown in Figure 7-2. The progression of measures from global performance to local indicators is shown from left to right. The first row deals with the business level. At the business level the customer measures and the global operational measures serve as performance indicators. From a detailed knowledge of customer and corporate expectations, and actual performance, one can identify the key performance factor needing improvement. From here one can identify the constraints and the relevant set of constraint measures. This is the same process that, when applied at the business level, leads to constraints and constraint measures.

The second row shows the application at the sub-unit level. We have chosen the level of a business unit. The performance of the business unit is provided by external and operational measures similar to the global measures. Gaps in the business unit performance drive the identification of key performance factors needing improvement. From here, using the constraint identification methodology, one can identify the "local constraint" as it relates to this specific business unit. Once the local constraints have been identified, appropriate measures can be developed. This set of measures becomes the focusing measures at the business unit level.

The third row shows the application to smaller sub-units such as departments and local (work center) activities. At this level it is possible that "global" measures do not make sense. One

Figure 7-2

Basic flow of logic in developing activity-focusing measures for various organizational levels.

Logical Progression				
Organizational Level	**Performance Measure**	**Key Performance Factor**	**Root Cause/ Constraint**	**Activity-focusing Measure**
Corporate or Division	Global In-Sync measures	Significant gap in performance	System constraint	System constraint measures
Business Unit	In-Sync measures	Gaps in sub-unit performance	Area or unit constraint	Unit constraint measures
Local Activity	Activity-outcome measures	Critical outcome	Activity constraint	Activity constraint measures

has to construct the appropriate activity-outcome measures. From here the process proceeds through key performance factors to "local constraint" identification to the activity-focusing measures.

In Figure 7-3, the table is filled out for a representative business. At the business level, starting with the global measures, expenses are identified as the key performance factor in need of improvement. On further analysis, it is determined that the division has far too many people to support the level of sales. However, it is difficult to reduce the work force due to lack of multiple skills among the operators. Thus, even though the work load at the lathe is less than 50 percent and at the drills is also less than 50 percent, this division must employ a lathe operator and a drill operator. Hence, the constraint measure is the skills matrix of the work force.

Figure 7-3

Examples of activity-focusing measures for various organizational levels.

Logical Progression				→
Organizational Level	**Performance Measure**	**Key Performance Factor**	**Root Cause/ Constraint**	**Activity-focusing Measure**
Division	Delivery, Quality, Price, etc., T, I, OE	OE	Labor flexibility	Skills matrix
Plant	Delivery, Quality, Price, etc., T, I, OE	I	Large process batch	Relative batch size
Shop department	Quality, Mix, Inventory, local OE	Mix	Changeover difficulty	Setup times

To show the progression to a lower level of the division we have chosen one of the plants. We have chosen a plant that has already implemented cross-training activities and in which OE is not the critical issue. This is not to say the plant can not improve on its spending. It means that the best way this plant can help the entire division is by reducing inventory. Inventory reduction at this plant has a larger impact on the division than achievable reductions in OE.

The key performance factor is thus identified as I. The question that this unit now asks is: *What is the constraint to reducing inventory?* This turns out to be the large process batches the plant uses due to setups at critical work centers. The activity-focusing measure becomes the batch size itself. As shown in

Figure 7-3, the batch size relative to the size of customer orders may be a measure that is easier to understand.

If one considers the department level in the plant, then the global performance measures may not make sense. This is the case shown in Figure 7-3. Activity-outcome measures are needed. Some activity-outcome type performance measures for this department include the quantity of production, the mix that was produced, quality, etc. This department must help the plant by working to reduce the batch sizes and hence inventory. This requirement reveals the setup time at key work centers as the activity-focusing measure.

As this example shows, the logic of constraint identification and management are applied to each subgroup within the organization. By making sure that the desired improvement at each level is tied through clear cause and effect connection to the business as a whole, local improvements do not conflict with one another. They are coordinated to leverage one another for the same global improvement.

Since business environments constantly change, all steps in this sequence should be frequently reviewed. Market conditions, removal of old constraints and new products and technologies can all change the characteristics of the business/operation. They can also change what is required from any individual step or process.

FOCUSED AND COORDINATED PROCESS OF CONTINUOUS IMPROVEMENT

In the approach outlined above, each operation will be evaluated using appropriate measures. Responsibility for assuring that the right set of measures is used falls on the local area managers. Process improvements are implemented after a two step check. First, one needs to make sure this improvement will have a significant impact on the activity-focusing measure. Then one must also make sure that this improvement in the activity-focusing measure will benefit the entire system. This approach is consistent with the synchronous approach of ensuring a true cause-effect relationship before action is taken.

The synchronous management process works as follows:

1. It all begins with managers making sure that the relationships of the business' various subsystems are well understood. This applies to all levels of the business, with each manager clearly understanding his or her area of responsibility. As business conditions, organizational structures, production processes, etc., change, it is management's responsibility to make sure that the nature of the relationships are constantly reevaluated, and that this understanding is shared by all members of their unit.

2. The next step is the constraint identification methodology. Using the performance expectations of the entire business as the target, specific performance factors that need improvement should be identified. This is a flow of information from the customer end to the supplier end of the business, with the higher level specifying the required improvements. The constraint identification methodology enables the proper identification of constraints — where they

are and what makes them constraints. This then enables the establishment of appropriate measures and improvement activities. Again, the nature and location of constraints, and hence the constraint measures, will be constantly changing. It is clearly the responsibility of area managers to keep abreast of changing circumstances (external and internal) and to ensure that the constraint identification methodology is continuously applied.

3. Each member of the unit should be encouraged to identify how he or she can contribute to improving the unit's performance. While a major portion of the manager's time and energy is focused on the constraint(s), he or she should coordinate the improvements in the non-constraints so as to maximize the cumulative impact of these changes.

All businesses, and manufacturing businesses in particular, are complex entities with complex dependencies. It is of primary importance that management make sure that all members of the organization understand the performance expectations. It is also the managers' responsibility to make sure that the interconnections between the different tasks performed by the various members are also clearly understood by all members. It is also management's responsibility to make all members aware of the impact each task has on the unit as a whole.

Everyone is then expected to assist in improving the team performance based on this understanding. When the interconnections between different sub-units are properly understood and the methodology is constantly applied to maintain relevance with changing situations, the synchronous approach provides focus and coordination to the continuous improvement process.

CHAPTER 8

CAPITAL INVESTMENT DECISIONS

Of all the practical applications of the new performance measurement system, one of the most important is reviewing capital appropriation requests. Certainly in today's economic environment this is an increasingly important issue. Companies simply do not have the luxury of making large capital purchases indiscriminately. Money is tight and traditional approaches to justify expenditures (i.e. standard cost calculations based on labor savings) fall short. As market conditions become less predictable — product life cycles get shorter, new models proliferate, upturns and downturns of the economy are shorter in duration and more difficult to predict — there is less certainty that investments will eventually pay off. The need for careful and wise investments is critical.

Every major capital investment must serve to support business goals at the strategic, tactical, and operational level. This is increasingly difficult without understanding the impact of an acquisition on the business *as a whole*, not just on the local department or area. The traditional approach is of little utility in accomplishing this. Clearly the In-Sync set of measures (with its link to the total business through the global measures and its focus on local constraints) provides better guidance for informed decisions on the likely impact an acquisition will have on overall business performance.

It should be noted that there may exist a multitude of legitimate business reasons for making capital investments which fall outside of any financial justification rationale. An example of this might be safety or environmental protection issues which must be addressed for the business to continue functioning effectively.

It has always been clearly understood that the objective of capital investments is to improve business performance. What has changed is the understanding of what "improved performance" means and the consequences of investing unwisely. The stable, mass production markets of yesterday were very forgiving of bad investments. If it took five or ten years for the actual payback to occur, all was not lost. The products and the equipment would still be around to realize the payback. This is no longer the case.

THE TRADITIONAL APPROACH

Before we examine the In-Sync approach to capital decision making it is important to understand where the traditional justification approach falls short. Under the traditional mindset (manufacturing is an efficiency machine) improved performance was immediately and clearly understood by everyone in the company. It was synonymous with improved labor utilization/efficiency. The standard cost-based justification process is based on the same faulty logic as the performance measures — labor costs drive everything else. If labor costs are reduced, it is assumed that the accompanying overhead and burden are reduced as well. The identified "savings" rarely materialize.

For example, it is left to the engineering departments of manufacturing companies to develop capital appropriation requests. The engineers will have some pre-defined guidelines, such as a two- or three-year "payback," for the acquisition of a specific piece of capital equipment. These guidelines are intended to provide an economic "cutoff" so that the organization will always realize the intended return. Most appropriation requests require substantially more detailed information, yet the underlying logic for calculating returns remains the same. The typical approach for calculating this payback is as follows:

Cost of proposed piece of equipment = $300,000
Part number to be produced = A12345
Labor standard on old equipment = 0.20 hours
Labor standard on proposed equipment = 0.10 hours
Cost per labor hour = $18.00
Overhead and burden multiplier = 300%
Cost of burdened labor hour = $72.00
Forecasted volume on P/N A12345 = 40,000 / year
Cost to produce on old equipment = $576,000
   (40,000 x 0.2 x $72.00)
Cost to produce on proposed equipment = $288,000
   (40,000 x 0.1 x $72.00)
Savings = $576,000 - $288,000 = $288,000
Payback on capital = Less than 2 years

This looks very straightforward and, based on the information provided, the decision would likely be made to purchase the proposed equipment. But would this be the right decision?

The calculation makes some questionable assumptions, which would not necessarily be apparent if viewed from the traditional perspective. Perhaps the most problematic is that the cost justification is based on fully burdened labor hours. The implicit assumption is that when the labor hours required to produce a specific product are cut back, all associated overhead functions are also eliminated. Our experience has shown that in the majority of organizations this is simply not the case.

It is critical to remember that the loading of labor hours with other costs is only a convention of convenience for the accounting community. It does not reflect any "basic truth" about the economics of a manufacturing business; it is only a method of allocating costs to specific products. A recurrent theme in this book has been the flawed assumptions arising from this convention and how they lead to poor, ill-informed decision making within manufacturing companies. Traditional capital justification thinking is an excellent example of this. Clearly, utilizing fully burdened labor hours to calculate "savings" is a flawed assumption. There are others.

For instance, another flawed assumption is that if the proposed piece of equipment is purchased, the corresponding level of direct labor will necessarily be eliminated. Historically, the assumption was that more would be produced and sold, thus reducing the unit cost of production. Since not all resources are bottlenecks this is not always true. If we look closely at the example, this potential "savings" represents a total of 4,000 man-hours per year. If we use an average of 1,750 hours per worker per year, this represents an equivalent savings of 2.3 workers. Even if we accept that the plant census will be reduced by some level, it will be somewhat difficult to layoff 0.3 of a worker.

SYNCHRONOUS APPROACH

The difference between the traditional approach and the synchronous approach starts with the difference in understanding what it means to "improve performance." In the synchronous mindset, improvements have to relate to improving the business' competitive position.

The central element in synchronous manufacturing thinking, as it relates to improving performance, is the concept of constraints. There are two related aspects to any changes, capital or otherwise.

The first relates to the question: *What is the impact on the system of this change?* Remember that in the highly interdependent world of business organizations this is not a trivial question.

The second aspect relates to an even more basic question: *Is the right problem being addressed?*

The answer to the first question can be obtained by relating local activities to the impact on the global measures. The answer to the second question is obtained through the constraint identification and management process.

WHAT IS THE IMPACT OF THIS CAPITAL PURCHASE?

The general process for calculating the impact of a new piece of equipment involves relating the capabilities of the new machine to T, I, and OE for the entire business.

To see how this is done, consider the previous example. Let us assume that the only change in process capability is that the new machine is faster; setup times, yields, skill level required, etc. stay the same. What is the impact on T, I, and OE if the new machine is installed?

We start by computing the impact on throughput. If the work center to be replaced is a bottleneck (or capacity constraint), speeding up this work center will result in greater production for the entire plant. This would be the case if demand for this product was more than 42,000 units (It takes 0.2 hours to produce one part. Therefore in one year — 50 weeks or 350 days — one can produce 42,000 units = 24 hrs x 350 days ÷ 0.2 hr/unit). It is immediately obvious that there is a major difference in the value of speeding up this process in the case when demand exceeds 42,000 units and when demand is less than 42,000 units.

1. Demand exceeds 42,000 units. Let's assume that the market demand for this product is 45,000 units. If the throughput per unit sold is $100 (note: this is sales price minus material cost), then the additional 3,000 units of production could translate to $300,000 in additional revenues. Note that actual production capability is 84,000 units with the new machine.

   The critical assumptions here are that there is demand for the additional units that can be produced, and that there are no other bottlenecks in the system — even at the increased rate of production. All other pieces of equipment are capable of producing 45,000 units.

2. Current demand is only 40,000 units. In this case, the resource is not a bottleneck to start with. The only way in which this resource can affect throughput is for it to provide the company with a competitive advantage. In other words, it can help improve the key competitive element such as quality or lead time sufficiently to boost sales. If this is the case, then the expected sales level should be obtained from sales personnel. If there are no other constraints to producing the additional units, then the new throughput estimate should be used to repeat the calculations in section 1 above.

If the new resource can not boost sales, then the additional production capability of the new machine is not needed. There is clearly no impact on plant throughput.

The next step is to calculate the impact on inventory. Here, it is important to understand the relationship between resources and product flow.

1. If demand exists for the additional units, then the inventory impact can be significant if the additional work begins to strain the reactive capacity of other work centers.

2. If the demand is for less than the 42,000 units, there is opportunity for lowering inventory. This is because the reactive capacity of this work center has been increased. How much inventory can be reduced will depend on the total flow and capacity map.

Finally, consider the impact on operating expenses. The new equipment will, most likely, change expenditures at the local level. The labor grade to operate the new equipment may be different; tooling requirements may be different; maintenance requirements may be different, and start up costs will be incurred, etc. In addition, the new equipment can influence other work centers. This impact will be different for the case of bottlenecks and non-bottlenecks.

1. If a bottleneck has been relieved and 3,000 additional units can be sold, the issue is whether additional capacity will be needed at other resources. This may be in the form of weekend or other overtime at work centers running five days a week or operating less than three shifts. The expense of this overtime will have to be considered.

2. If the work center is not a bottleneck, the impact on operating expense will be limited to the impact at this work center.

Once the impact on T, I, and OE has been calculated, an evaluation of the investment can be made. For example, if the investment relieved a constraint and resulted in additional sales (case 1 above), with an impact of $70,000 in overtime expenses at some other work centers and minimal impact on inventory — the additional revenues (after material cost) of $300,000 would be compared with the increased expenses of $70,000 per year and the investment cost of $300,000. It would appear to be a good investment.

It is clear that there are no real benefits if the investment does not boost sales, despite the calculations of the standard cost system. Then this would not be a wise investment.

QUESTIONS TO REMEMBER
WHEN LOOKING AT INVESTMENTS

Obviously the traditional standard cost approach to capital justification is based around a local, rather than global, perspective of the business. Without a thorough, detailed understanding of the complex interactions of all the resources within a manufacturing environment, it is extremely difficult to identify "savings." The synchronous measures serve to provide a framework in which the impact of a capital acquisition can be understood, not at the local level, but rather from a system-wide perspective. What will the impact be on throughput, on inventory, and on operating expense?

This necessarily will lead to a different set of questions that need to be addressed in the justification process. It is certainly more realistic to calculate these numbers to identify the potential impact of a new piece of equipment, than it would be to approach the decision from a labor savings direction only. Following is a set of questions that should be answered to understand the overall impact of a specific investment. Every appropriation request should consider the answers to these questions.

Throughput-related questions:

1. Is market demand currently being met?
   - If not, will it be met with this appropriation?
   - If market demand is currently being met, will more throughput be generated? How much and when?
   - Are all future requirements included in this analysis?

2. Will the proposed equipment be utilized at a currently constrained resource?
   - If not, where will the proposed resource be relative to the existing constraint (in the product routing)?
   - What will be the impact on flow to or after the constraint?
   - What will be the impact on current lead times?
   - Will queue time at the constrained resource be reduced?

3. Can more work be brought into the unit as a result of purchasing this equipment (i.e. offload from other areas, new parts, other business opportunities)?

Inventory-related questions:

4. What will be the net impact of the proposed equipment on material flow and corresponding inventory levels?

5. Will the proposed equipment be incorporated into the plant layout to facilitate the physical product flow?

6. What work centers are likely to lose reactive capacity, and what is the anticipated impact on lead times and inventory?

Operating Expense-related questions:

7. What will be the impact of the purchase on human resources?
   - In the direct labor force?
   - In support areas such as the tool room, maintenance, programming?

8. What is the plan for, and cost of, initial and ongoing training (operators, maintenance, engineering, electronics, etc.)?
   - Has a formal training program been developed?
   - Are training costs additional to equipment acquisition?

9. What will be the impact of this equipment on tooling costs?
   - What are the start-up tooling costs?
   - What are the estimated future durable tooling costs?
   - Are significant amounts of tooling to be made obsolete due to this appropriation?

10. What is monthly depreciation and expenses for equipment over the first three years?

11. Are the equipment features specified necessary for production (all options needed)?

Another aspect of new equipment is its potential for disruptions. Remember that disruptions affect T, I, and OE.

12. Will the machine have a high reliability?
    - Has maintenance provided lead times and subsequent costs associated with spare parts inventory necessary for this equipment?
    - What is the life expectancy of this equipment at the proposed rate of utilization?
    - Does the manufacturer guarantee that spare parts will be available for the expected lifetime of the equipment?
    - Will external personnel be required for any routine maintenance?
    - Does the manufacturer offer a preventive maintenance program?

Finally, the alternatives to buying the new machinery must be considered:

13. Can changing operating procedures achieve the same results (i.e. setup improvement, yield, lot sizing, work rules, shift staffing)?

14. Can the product be manufactured on existing equipment within other departments or business units? On modified existing equipment? Using alternate technologies?

15. Can work be performed by an external vendor?
   - If yes, at what cost?
   - With what effect on current lead times?
   - With what effect on current inventory levels?

Some other pertinent questions that should always be considered in evaluating new equipment include:

16. What will be the impact on overall process capabilities?

17. Does the proposed resource fit within existing standardization strategies?
   - Operating and scheduling policies?
   - Standardized tooling and fixtures?
   - Integration with other equipment (CNC programming, controllers)?
   - Current skill levels of labor force?

18. What is the equipment manufacturer's performance in product quality? In relative cost? In providing service? Delivery performance to schedule?

19. Is this equipment a guaranteed "turn-key" installation?

20. Is the proposed equipment sensitive to obsolescence and technological changes?

21. How long will it take from receipt of equipment to full production capabilities?

This list is obviously intended to provide management with a very detailed analysis of the potential impact of a capital acquisition on the total business. Some of these areas may not pertain specifically to some business environments, yet the overall intention is universal: what is the impact on throughput, inventory, and operating expense likely to be? The ability to understand this will lead to significantly better decision making.

The questioning process enables managers to calculate the true impact of specific investment decisions on the entire business. The aforementioned example shows the return on the investment of $300,000 in the new machine. What this does not show is if this is the best choice among several alternatives. For this a process is needed to rank-order alternative investments.

IS THIS TARGETED AT THE RIGHT PROBLEM?

The process of establishing activity-focusing and constraint measures is the starting point for a capital investment decision. The key to improving business performance is to enhance the performance of constraints. Business-level constraints have the most impact, while local constraints have a much smaller impact on the total business. It should be clear that the capital investment decision process (i.e. decision to invest in equipment, buildings, etc.) is a subset of the improvement decision process. This general process in the synchronous approach involves the following steps:

Step 1:   List the business constraints.

Since constraints are the limiting factors to performance, the starting point is a clear listing. Also, remember that constraints are not limited to equipment or machinery and could be in logistical or policy aspects of the business. The capital investment decisions would be limited to those constraints that require capital expenditures for their removal.

Step 2:   Identify what is needed to enhance constraint performance.

This step identifies what specifically needs to be done to improve performance. The activity-focusing measure has indicated which outcome must be improved. This step is aimed at identifying the step in the process that must be improved and identifies the improvement necessary.

Step 3:   Calculate the impact of enhancing/removing the constraint.

This begins the financial justification or decision process. If the investment is made and the constraint addressed, then what is the true impact on the entire business? The answer to this question lies in understanding the impact on the T, I, and OE of the business.

Step 4:   Rank-order the multitude of investment opportunities.

The logical choice among the alternatives (all things being equal) would be the one with the maximum impact on the entire business. The synchronous process reveals the true impact of any changes to the manufacturing/distribution chain. At this point the potential benefits of the decision are clear.

By using this systematic approach capital will be invested where it can impact the entire business the most.

CHAPTER 9

PRODUCT COST & PRODUCT MIX DECISIONS

That one should "know" what it costs to produce a particular item if one wishes to run a profitable operation is a specious idea. Assigning unit costs through a well-defined allocation process is one of the more important applications of the standard cost system.

It is clear why a manager wants to know costs on a per-unit basis. The logic is as follows:

- Profits are clearly the difference between sales revenues and expenses. Every product sold generates revenue and costs money to produce. If we can make sure that a profit is made on each unit, the entire business will make a profit.

- It is easy to calculate the revenue side for each unit; it is the price of that unit. If, somehow, the cost side can be determined precisely, the price can be set so that each unit sold generates a profit. Additionally, it will be possible to maximize corporate profit by weeding out products that cost more than a company can reasonably charge, and focusing on products that generate larger profit margins.

In keeping with the traditional mindset, this way of looking at product cost and product mix has a high internal bias; the focus is on the cost of production. But today, business leaders and managers are increasingly coming to the realization that the standard cost system does not effectively identify true or real costs of production, many of which are tied up with the system's constraints.

Let's take the example of a company that manufactures a product line of bar seats. Some basic information about the company includes:

- 3 shifts, 5-days-a-week operation (24 hrs/day), 22-day month.
- one worker, V, and one worker, W, per shift, not interchangeable.
- labor cost is $6.00 per hour.
- total operating expenses of the plant = $12,672 per month.
- material is infinitely available.
- no lost production time for lunch or breaks.
- no changeover time.

The product line includes four seats, which sell for varying prices and take different amounts of each worker's time to produce, all shown in Figure 9-1.

The problem is to determine the appropriate mix of the four different seats to maximize profit. The marketing department feels that the "full line" is a necessity, even though it has no problem with emphasizing the profitable products more heavily. The quantitative expression of this market constraint is that the manufacturing operation must make at least one unit of the "less profitable" products for every ten of the profitable ones. The mix can not be skewed by more than a factor of 10 to 1.

Using the standard cost system, the decision would be to make 10 of each of the basic models for every one of the deluxe models. This is a rather simple calculation, since the labor and

Figure 9-1

Schematic diagram of products made by the Bar Seat Company.

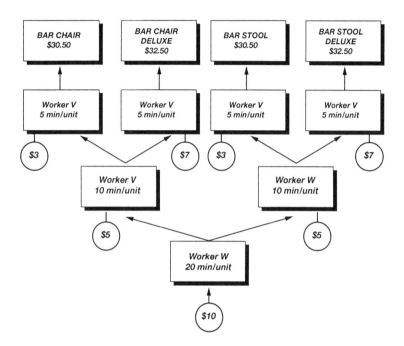

overhead are equal for all four models, and the only difference in "cost" is that the materials for the deluxe models are more expensive. Standard cost calculations are shown in Figures 9-2 and 9-3.

The desired ratio of the four models (see Figure 9-3), 10:1:10:1, is called a "ship set." The next question to consider is how many such sets can be made and shipped in a given month. The constraint on the number of ship sets that can be produced in any month is clearly the amount of time worker W must put in. Looking back at Figure 9-1 we see that for each ship set, worker W must put in 550 minutes = (20 minutes each x 10 bar

Figure 9-2

Product costs as calculated by the standard cost system.

Product	Bar Chair	Bar Chair Deluxe	Bar Stool	Bar Stool Deluxe
Labor	$3.50	$3.50	$3.50	$3.50
Material	$18.00	$22.00	$18.00	$22.00
Overhead	$3.50	$3.50	$3.50	$3.50
Total	$25.00	$29.00	$25.00	$29.00

Figure 9-3

Preferred products as selected by the standard cost system.

Product	Bar Chair	Bar Chair Deluxe	Bar Stool	Bar Stool Deluxe
Selling Price	$30.50	$32.50	$30.50	$32.50
Cost	$25.00	$29.00	$25.00	$29.00
Profit	$5.50	$3.50	$5.50	$3.50
Desired Ratio	10:	1:	10:	1:

chairs) + (20 minutes x 1 bar chair deluxe) + (30 minutes x 10 bar stools) + (30 minutes x 1 bar stool deluxe). Worker V must put in 220 minutes to produce the same mix. In the 31,680 minutes he and worker V work in a standard month, only 57.6 ship sets can be completed, so 57 can be completed and shipped.

So the profit calculation looks like this:

Monthly sales revenue
= $38,475
= ([10 x $30.50] + $32.50 + [10 x $30.50] + $32.50) x 57 ship sets
Cost of material = $23,028
= ($180 + $22 + $180 + $22) x 57 ship sets
Expenses (OE) = $12,672
Total Cost = $35,700
Gross Margin = $2,775, or a 7.2 percent return on sales.

Using the synchronous methodology, the question is which product contributes the most to the company's financial goals within the framework of the existing constraints? In other words, how is throughput maximized for the given expenses.

Remember, throughput is determined by the bottleneck in the facility — more precisely by the time available at the bottleneck. Products that generate the most throughput per hour of the bottleneck make the most contribution to total throughput and hence to profits. The profitability of each product can be determined by calculating:

Profitability = $\dfrac{\text{Contribution to Throughput}}{\text{Time at the constraint}}$

Figure 9-4

Preferred products as calculated by the Synchronous approach.

Product	Bar Chair	Bar Chair Deluxe	Bar Stool	Bar Stool Deluxe
Throughput T (= selling price minus material)	$12.50	$10.50	$12.50	$10.50
Minutes of constraint per unit	20	20	30	30
T per constraint minute	$0.63	$0.53	$0.42	$0.35
Desired ratio	10:	1:	1:	1:

In this case, the constraint is W, and it takes W more time to work on either a bar stool or bar stool deluxe than on a bar chair or bar chair deluxe. Hence, the calculation seen in Figure 9-4, and the desired ratio is 10:1:1:1.

Resource W's required time to produce a ship set with a 10:1:1:1 ratio is 280 minutes (= [10 x 20 minutes] + 20 + 30 + 30), and in the standard 31,680-minute month, he can produce 113.14 ship sets, so 113 can be built and shipped.

Under the synchronous methodology, the profit calculation looks like this:

Monthly sales revenue
$$= \$45{,}256.50$$
$$= ([10 \times \$30.50] + \$32.50 + \$30.50 + \$32.50)$$
x 113 ship sets

Cost of materials
$$= \$27{,}346$$
$$= (\$180 + \$22 + \$18 + \$22) \times 113 \text{ ship sets}$$

Expenses (OE) = $ 12,672 (fixed)

Total Expenses = $ 40,018

Gross Margin = $ 5,238.50, or an 11.6 percent return on sales.

As this example shows, the "cost" of a constraint is more than the dollars and cents of labor or materials. As we explore the issues of product costing and determining the appropriate product mix in more detail, a number of different constraints and the impact they have on the cost calculations will be apparent.

TYPICAL PROBLEMS WITH THE TRADITIONAL APPROACH

Beyond the inability to recognize constraints, there are also a number of problems that occur from the standard cost system's focus on calculating direct labor and then "burdening" that labor with overhead through a "peanut buttering" of indirect costs across product lines. Some of those problems are:

- the subsidizing of special and small-run products by standard products, since standard products get very little attention from engineering and very little benefits from the other costs that are allocated across all products.

- excessive proliferation of product lines, since complexity is not recognized and/or not included in computing initial product costs. Consider for example offering more color combinations. A product of a different color may have the same direct labor time. Addition of the new color would not change the cost of the existing products and the "cost" of the new product would appear to be the same. The increase in product offering, however, does add complexity that adds real costs to the "indirect" category of costs, and hence to the costs of all products.

- favoring automation or capital solutions over cheaper, more flexible but more labor-intensive solutions. The standard cost system does not distinguish between constraints and non-constraints in the manufacturing system. Hence the impact of product mix is seriously underestimated.

The most fundamental problem of the standard cost system in this regard is its inability to recognize manufacturing as an interdependent system. It looks for margin at the individual unit level in isolation. It does not take into account changes, in volume or in any individual product, that can have an impact on the cost of running the entire system, and hence the cost of producing each and every unit of every product made.

Since the early 1980s, a partial remedy has been found. Activity-Based Costing, or ABC, seeks to remove problems created when direct labor is used as the basis for allocations. It attempts to apportion the cost of both direct labor and indirect/overhead costs directly to the product or production process. In this way, true organizational efforts undertaken for any product can be identified. But ABC still suffers from the failure to recognize the level of manufacturing interactions, and from the failure to differentiate between constraints and non-constraints.

SYNCHRONOUS APPROACH TO PRODUCT COST

In looking at the issue of product costs, we propose an approach to answer two basic questions:

1. *Should the company accept a contract or price for a specific product?*

2. *Can the company restructure its current product mix in order to increase profitability?*

ACCEPTING NEW BIDS/JOBS

Remember that it is not enough to make a profit on a particular contract in a vacuum. The first question a manufacturing manager must ask in determining whether to accept a new contract is: *What impact will accepting this order have on our ability to meet current customer commitments?* Each new contract or business can have an impact on the company's ability to meet current customer commitments in a number of ways:

1. Existing capacity may be insufficient to deal with the additional business. The new work may create new bottlenecks, or may exacerbate bottlenecks that already exist. Even if the new contract is more profitable than current contracts, it is important to know whether current orders would be delayed as a result of capacity bottlenecks.

One real life example is a company that makes industrial containers. The plant manufactures both aluminum and steel containers. Based on the calculation of margins, it was determined that aluminum containers are more profitable and should be promoted over steel containers. The sales force did precisely this, and the product mix shifted from mostly steel to mostly aluminum.

The change in product mix dramatically changed the load on certain resources. The heat treat furnaces unexpectedly emerged as bottlenecks. By the time the problem was even clearly identified, inventory had climbed dramatically, poor deliveries were jeopardizing all sales, and costs in the form of reactionary overtime and offloading were running amuck.

2. The additional load may strain the plant's reactive capacity. Even if no bottlenecks are created, any additional load will consume capacity that was available to respond to disruptions and hence to meet existing customer commitments. With the loss of any reactive capacity, lead times tend to get longer; how much longer is the key issue. If these lead times begin to affect current customer satisfaction and have a negative impact on the current level of throughput, then there is clearly a strain on reactive capacity.

Consider, for example, a resource that has a history of being unreliable (too many breakdowns). If the average time to recover from a breakdown is four hours and the average load on the machine is six hours per day (assuming one eight-hour shift) then the machine can recover (i.e. get back on schedule) in two days. If the additional work increases the load to seven hours per day, then the time to recover increases to four days. It doubles!

3. The new business may have an impact on material availability. It can divert material from existing buffer stocks, or it may

strain the ability of suppliers to gear up. If the impact on material supply is ignored, misallocation of materials and shortages are likely to occur.

Clearly, in the highly interdependent world of manufacturing, accepting new orders can have an impact on the current flow of product to the marketplace. This impact needs to be carefully considered before proceeding with the financial side of the picture.

Once a customer-based review is done, the financial side of accepting the order needs to be examined. This should start by computing the impact of the new business on T, I, and OE.

First, with the contract price — or maximum competitive price for the product — the throughput generated for the entire system with the additional order will have to be computed with recognition of system constraints. In other words, the new and real T will have to be computed.

If capacity and/or material constraints are involved, then the new business may be at the expense of some existing business. In this case it can not be assumed that the new revenue is additional revenue. Some of it is substituted for revenue lost from the old business. If policy constraints — such as head counts, overtime, etc. — are involved, then relaxing the constraint may have a positive impact on all customers. These factors will have to be reviewed and taken into account.

Second, the impact of accepting and producing the new order on total operating expenses must be computed. One must look for true increases in expenses and not just the incremental increase in work load. As an example, non-bottleneck work centers may be able to handle the additional work without additional resources or even overtime. At these resources there would be no increase in expenses. Total OE, with and without the new business, must be computed.

Consider first the case when there are no constraints before and after the new order is accepted. In this case, the new production can be accomplished with existing resources. No additional expenses are involved. The only additional outlay of money will be to purchase the materials used to make the finished product, the components and raw materials used in the product's fabrication and assembly.

Every unit sold will incur only the additional purchase of materials, and will not involve any expenses for resources (until a constraint emerges). Each unit sold will contribute the full throughput value (selling price minus material cost) to the bottom line.

If constraints are involved, then the production of this new product will be at the expense of another product. In this case each unit sold will contribute to the bottom line its throughput value minus the throughput value of the product it displaces.

Once the total expected production is known, the increase in expenses can be computed by identifying the additional resources required. It is important to underscore the point that one is to look for the true additional capacity purchased. Unlike the standard cost system, which assumes all work to constitute additional costs, the synchronous methodology recognizes that non-constraint resources can perform a certain amount of additional work without additional expenses in the form of overtime or additional workers.

Finally, the impact on inventory must be determined. The

largest impact of inventory changes will be felt on ROA and cash flow. New business can affect inventory in two ways. First, material will be needed to satisfy the new order, and will be in the system for some times. In addition to this direct impact, the new business may have an impact on total inventories by changing the reactive capacity, and hence the lead time. Both factors need to be recognized. The effects of these changes in inventory are most severe if cash flow effects are critical and may influence the acceptance of the order, or at least payment terms.

With the complete picture of the impact on all elements of the In-Sync set in hand, the actual decision making process should be straightforward. This is not to say that the correct decision will be self-evident or that multiple "what if" scenarios will not have to be analyzed. Trade-offs may still have to be reviewed and judgment calls made. The crucial point is that decisions will be made after reviewing the total impact of accepting the new order.

PRODUCT MIX ISSUES

The critical issue here is whether the mix of products produced matches the production capabilities. The Bar Seat Company example showed how synchronous concepts work when dealing with bottlenecks or capacity constraints. The example below illustrates how the concepts work when dealing with complex issues of yields, changeover times, run speeds, etc.

The key production processes involved in the manufacture of a particular product are printing and forming. The print design on each product is unique to the individual customer, while the forms tend to fall into a predetermined set. Superb print capability is the company's key competitive advantage.

To secure business from a new customer, the company has to compete with other, lower-quality producers. Figure 9-5 shows the relative range of costs for the various products as calculated by the standard cost system. Note that we have grouped the products into four major categories — simple to print, simple to form; simple to print, complex to form; complex to print, simple to form; complex to form, complex to print. The range is fairly limited, and predictably, this company can not compete on the low end but is the preferred choice for the complex to print, complex to form category.

When we examine the same product mix from a synchronous view the cost differential for the various products shows a much larger variation, with a six-fold difference in cost, as shown in Figure 9-6. This reflects the true costs of the complex items, both in the design phase, the prototype phase, and the actual production phase. The complex products require much longer setup times. Yields are lower, and

Figure 9-5

Range of costs for various products using the standard cost approach.

		Forming Difficulty	
		Low	High
Print Difficulty	Low	1.0	1.2
	High	1.2	1.5

the run speeds at both forming and printing are significantly slower. The slower speed is the major factor recognized by the standard cost system. The In-Sync set weighs the costs with the recognition that printing is the potential constraint. This means that the value of an hour at printing is tied to system throughput and not just to the machine or labor costs.

Figure 9-6

Range of costs for various products using the Synchronous approach.

	Forming Difficulty	
	Low	**High**
Low	1.0	1.8
High	4.0	6.0

Print Difficulty (vertical axis label)

Clearly, the company is undercharging on complex products and overcharging on simple products. The most important thing to emerge from this exercise — done jointly with design, production and sales — is the shared understanding that simple changes in print pattern, for example, cause major changes in the degree of difficulty for manufacturing, and hence major changes in the cost. By involving design engineers before the product quotes are developed, simple changes acceptable to the customer can be created, resulting in significant price and competitive advantage.

SOME TYPICAL APPLICATIONS

There are a number of frequent applications or uses for the "unit cost" concept.

1. Review of product line profitability

This is the exercise illustrated at the beginning of this chapter. It clearly highlights the inadequacies of the traditional approach. Although the concept of bottleneck contribution serves as a useful tool in comparing two different products, the key point is that products can not be looked at in isolation. Product A can not be removed from the mix without affecting the expenses involved in the production of products B, C, etc. The impact of adding or removing each product from the mix will have to be examined by understanding the impact on T, I, and OE for each decision. Knowledge of constraints and the general characteristics of the specific operation can be used to develop quick rules of thumb to make these evaluations.

2. Rationalizing Production Operations

When there are multiple plants within a division capable of producing the same products, the question of deciding which plant should produce which products takes on some significance. The heart of the traditional approach is to compare production costs for various products at the different plants. As we have seen, this unit cost-based approach is not conducive to valid business decisions.

In the synchronous approach, the natural selection process is to assign production to specific plants in accordance with the capability to provide the best service to customers.

Only if there are overwhelming advantages to be gained by grouping on the basis of some other criteria (such as part geometry, process technology, etc.) would one desire to deviate from the customer-driven choice.

Every product removed from a plant or added to a plant has an impact on customer service levels. The impact on T, I, and OE must also be calculated, as outlined above. With this comprehensive picture intelligent decisions can begin to be made.

3. Make/Buy decisions

Should the company manufacture a particular part in its own factory or buy it from an outside source? The traditional approach again has been to compare the unit cost of production in-house to the price charged by an outside supplier.

The most damaging distortion created by the standard cost system is the allocation of indirect expenses across all products. Most often this allocation is based on direct labor hours and does not bear any correlation to the actual time or effort expended by the indirect resource toward the product.

For example, a mature product on which very little engineering work is done still carries a significant share of the total engineering expenses. In this way some products are subsidized and others charged more than their fair share. This type of allocation system is a prime reason why most large firms feel that they can not compete with the "garage down the street" in the production of mature, simple products. The unit cost at the plant carries the full overhead, while the unit cost at the garage has no extraneous expenses to allocate!

In the synchronous approach, the decision to buy a part from an outside supplier must be made by evaluating the true savings in OE against the total costs of buying the part from the supplier. The throughput for the system is affected by the change in material content of the finished product (since the raw material price and the purchased price will most likely be different). Inventory may change — material may have to be stocked if the supplier is a long distance away or is unreliable; it may go down if the supplier is very responsive or is willing to manage it on a consignment basis. Finally, operating expenses may change if the labor force can be reduced, support services reduced (or increased to handle the more complex logistics), and so on.

The changes in T, I, and OE will give the full picture of the impact of this decision to outsource a specific product. Customer and competitive impact, along with the impact on the operation (as measured by T, I, and OE), form the rational basis for the decision.

The same reasoning is applied when evaluating whether to insource a part currently purchased. It should be evident that the synchronous approach and the standard system are most likely to result in very different answers to the question of sourcing. In large complex organizations, the standard system will be biased in favor of outsourcing, since the allocation will spread the full costs across all products. The synchronous view looks at each outsourcing and insourcing decision at the margin and will tend to favor insourcing.

CHAPTER 10

KEY IMPLEMENTATION ISSUES

While the need to change measurements is intuitive to many leaders, both at the corporate and operating level, implementing the new measurements is often more difficult than implementing changes in operating methods. For most of the organization, especially non-financial people, the direct linkage between the business' profitability and the traditional measures set has always been assumed. Questioning the validity of this fundamental assumption will create a great deal of organizational anxiety. Many individuals will have moved up the ranks fueled by their "success" with the old criteria. It follows that these individuals will resist changing these criteria.

T, I, and OE measures speak directly to making money and to satisfying customers. As a result, at senior levels in most organizations, there is general willingness to embrace In-Sync type measures. Resistance to changing the basic scheme for making daily decisions is more prevalent at the lower organizational levels. But the apparent willingness to change at even the senior levels masks a number of issues that arise in all implementations of new measurement systems. Among them are:

1. Methods changes usually precede measurement system changes. Many times senior managers agree to methods changes and tell operating managers, "Don't worry about the numbers; I know the methods changes will make the numbers look bad to start." This attitude can set everyone involved up for misunderstandings and trouble in the future.

Without a firm commitment from the top to measure the results of methods changes in a different way, line workers, supervisors and operating managers fear that they will continue to be measured in the old way regardless of the assurance "not to worry." Consequently, they don't put all their efforts into implementing the methods changes and don't achieve the results they should, and the numbers "look bad."

Or the people at the operating level give it their all only to find that the senior manager who told them not to worry did not have support from the top. That manager gets heat about the bad numbers, which he or she transfers to the operating-unit personnel, who feel sandbagged — and rightly so.

2. This new measurement system asks everyone, from supervisors and operating managers on up, to "be a businessman." Instead of being focused narrowly on the standard cost system and the ratios on which they have been judged in the past, these individuals have to take a more comprehensive view of manufacturing activities and become versed in more of the complexities of the business.

Some of the actions that make sense under the In-Sync measures may appear to be foolhardy under standard cost measures. People will be reluctant to initiate these actions unless they are convinced they will be allowed to make mistakes without being harshly penalized. They also need to feel that everyone is working under the same set of measurements and sharing in the perceived risk.

3. Hand-in-hand with the new measures should come a realization that budgeting will be done in an entirely different way. Manufacturing operations will operate to a macro budget — gross annual throughput will equal X, manufactured for Y cost.

The goal of the operating manager should be to more closely match production with actual customer demand so as to attain sales (or more precisely, throughput) rather than just production (which may sit on the shelves as inventory). In turn this requires that the local operating manager have full flexibility to use his or her human, capital, and purchased material resources appropriately, rather than in the rigid fashion they were forced to do under the old-fashioned line-item budgeting. The dynamic world of manufacturing necessitates flexibility within specific financial guidelines. Maintenance of a specific T/OE ratio provides this flexibility while maintaining margins.

4. It is always important to remember that the intention of making these changes is to bring the internal methods, measures and mindsets into line with the external realities of the market. Clearly, any effort that neglects these critical elements will ultimately fail.

It is important to understand that the "three-legged stool" (measures, methods, and mindset) can not stand unless all three are aligned and are self-consistent. It would certainly be a mistake to attempt to utilize a standard cost-based measurement approach within an environment implementing synchronous manufacturing methods. The messages that the measures would send to the organization would be completely counter-productive from a synchronous perspective. Unfortunately, there exists very little "middle ground" on which these divergent systems coexist. This situation only highlights the importance of organizational commitment to discarding out-dated, dysfunctional approaches and embracing the new, more appropriate systems for today's market realities.

ORGANIZING A TEAM TO CREATE NEW MEASURES

In our experience, a serious drawback of traditional performance measurements is the lack of ownership by the people measured. Manufacturing personnel generally feel that they have little input into the definition of the measures. They also have little understanding of how most of the indicators are calculated, find little guidance for future activities from the measures, and are in general resigned to management's use of performance measurements as a "stick" and not as a management tool. Measurement systems have been more focused on **where the company has been** rather than **where the company is going.**

We use a process to design and implement a new set of measurements that is specific in its attempt to foster understanding of the measurements, achieve consensus about their use and create ownership and buy-in from the outset. The most effective way to achieve this is to work through a carefully constructed team that has regular, structured and focused meetings. Participation in the definition and development activities associated with the new measures is the singular key to their long-term success.

This new measures team should have representation from most disciplines and levels of the organization, with a total membership of between five and fifteen. Members should be selected from production, finance, marketing and sales, engineering, information systems, and other appropriate areas. The team's objectives must be clearly established by senior management and equally clearly communicated to the entire organization. This objective is best defined in the form of a mission statement that defines goals, scope, and timetables. Once defined, the mission statement should be given wide distribution within the organization.

A relatively high-level representative from divisional or corporate finance should also sit on the team. This is necessary to ensure that the outcome will be acceptable to operating and financial management at the corporate and/or divisional level. The plant's operating managers need assurance that financial management is in agreement with the changes in performance measurement — not just in principle but in the details. Furthermore, this individual can help the group to more clearly understand the relationship between the new measures and the business' financial health. This should serve to provide greater clarity through the design process for the non-financial members of the team.

The level of buy-in by the company's financial community is another critical success factor in both the development and implementation of the new measures set. Our experience is that generally most controllers and other top financial officers have a good understanding of the problems associated with the traditional cost-based system and are more than willing to participate in the development of alternate approaches.

The Institute of Management Accountants has published volumes of material relating the weaknesses of the cost accounting system (and associated allocation schemes) and is generally supportive of the type of performance measures discussed in this book. (For more information, contact the Institute of Management Accountants, 10 Paragon Drive, Montvale, NJ 07645-1760, (201) 573-9000.) Our experience is that the controller is often the most vocal supporter of the change effort.

The team should be chaired by a senior operating executive. The time and energy senior executives are willing to commit is a direct indication of their willingness to carry through the change effort. The chairperson must attend all committee meetings, take an active part in the meetings, and demonstrate commitment by removing obstacles through direct intervention on behalf of the team.

Clearly, senior management participation and support of any effort is required for success. If the initial attitude is one of acquiescence as opposed to active support, the effort is likely to fail. The team chair serves the vital function of demonstrating visible support for the changes to the balance of the organization. The level of credibility this individual has within the company will reflect directly on the team and their mission. It is always important to remember that the changes engendered in the measures strike at the heart of the organization's mindset.

Most individuals will have progressed through the company by performing "well" using the old set of measures. By taking this away, one will create a substantial level of uncertainty and stress. Senior management's active, visible role in the change effort provides some level of comfort. An additional role for the team will be to provide guidance and education concerning the criteria for success within the context of the newly defined measures. It is important that operating personnel have a detailed understanding of the types of behavior required to be successful in the new environment.

The team will probably be in effect for between twelve and twenty-four months (one to two full years). It takes most companies between four and eight months to complete the task of developing a new measures set, and the team should remain in place for at least six months to help managers as they make the transition to the new metrics.

DESIGNING THE NEW MEASUREMENT SYSTEM AND PROCESS

During the time the team is actually designing the new system, its meetings will be frequent, with enough time between meetings to accomplish assigned small-group or individual tasks. Many companies find that open "brainstorming"-type meetings work best, then summarizing the meetings' outcomes and assigning more detailed tasks highlighted during the meetings to individuals and small groups.

The team's task is to take the framework presented in this book and construct a set of measures that is tailored to its specific company. Adding and deleting elements that make up the measures set and the exact definitions of the elements is a necessary exercise to make sure that the measures set constructed is tailored to the company's unique needs. Also bear in mind that the measures will, in all likelihood, change with time.

As the team goes about developing a customized structured set of measures, the objective of the measures should always remain in the forefront. The measures must be constantly subjected to the following series of validation questions:

1. Can each level in the organization relate local activities and improvements to the business needs of the entire company?

2. Do the measures focus on the critical competitive elements affecting the marketplace?

3. Do the measures send a clear signal about what is important to accomplish?

4. Is the design of the measures set a top-down design? (i.e. Are we starting at the business level and working our way down to the lower levels so we won't lose relevance?)

5. Are the measures vertically and horizontally integrated?

The team's primary task is to take the key measurements discussed in this book (customer satisfaction, competitive performance, operational performance, and local indicators) and develop specific detailed definitions applicable to the company, and then to develop procedures for implementing the measures. For example, a committee will have to get to the level of defining computations such as:

Defining Raw Material Inventory

Value assigned: the purchased part value of the material. No labor or other charges are included.
Source of data: Financial standard cost file.
Quantity: The material included in this category is all of the material held in rough stores (location XXX and YYY), plus castings, forgings, and other semi-finished materials. (Note that castings and forgings that are transformed by machining may be included in raw materials, but brackets and bearings that are not transformed may be considered as component inventory.)

The level of detail involved in defining the specific measures is often daunting. It is necessary that the team understand the importance of such detailed calculations in order to assure consistency of logic and purpose. Obviously, there are specific reasons for the exclusion of labor from inventory valuations that relate to the way individual costs are perceived. Such details will present numerous opportunities for debate and discussion among committee members. This is all part of the process of developing ownership and understanding.

In addition, the team will design the report format, which should be as short as possible yet complete, so as to be useful to immediate users. The tendency in manufacturing companies is to make the report all-inclusive, which often results in numerous indices and voluminous, cumbersome reports.

One company utilized over fifty performance indicators on a weekly basis. This was presented in a six-page report that used an extremely confusing format. Further, the formulas used were mysterious at best and suspect at worst. The utility of such a document in helping operating personnel to manage is minimal. There existed no buy-in to these measures at any level of the organization. The measures accomplished the exact opposite of their original intent. Simplicity in design and presentation will facilitate both understanding as well as the active use of the measures in conducting day-to-day activities.

FROM DESIGN TO USAGE

Once the new system is designed, there will be a time of transition before it is fully installed. The team should remain in effect during this period, meeting far less frequently. The committee should be used as an arbitrator in working out bugs, or defining nuances that become apparent during actual day-to-day usage.

It must be agreed up-front that the new system will be the only one used once it is designed, that it will not be a parallel system used in conjunction with the old system. There will always be disagreements, misunderstandings, and questions about the applicability of the new measures in specific circumstances.

There will also be a tendency for some managers to continue computing the old measure and to bash the new system when it diverges from the old.

The team's voice and authority will usually be more powerful in getting people to reach agreement on contentious issues than will the voices of individuals, especially since those individuals may be on one side or the other of any issue. Senior managers may also have to be restrained from reverting back to the comfort zone of the old measures. This is one of the critical areas where the organization of the committee is crucial. The membership, in seniority and credibility, should be such that they can realign senior management's behavior as well.

While the team is retained as an arbitration panel of sorts, management has some strenuous tasks to accomplish during the transitional period. It must make the new measurement system available to all its operating managers and must educate them on the effective undertaking of an operational review under the new system and use of the reports. It must also guide and teach operational managers as they communicate throughout the organization that the old system is "dead and buried."

In all of these endeavors **communication** is the key to success. While the in-process set of measures may not see widespread distribution, the end results must. Minutes of the meetings should be published on a regular basis, with clear summaries of any decisions reached. Once the package itself has been defined and designed, a sample should be produced and distributed. This should include all the definitions of the variables, a key defining the calculations themselves and any other relevant information.

Business performance measures must be translated to individual performance measures, and recognition and incentives must be given to those who meet goals set under the new performance measures rather than the old ones.

Finally, the performance measurement process needs to be aligned with the whole variety of business processes in order to be fully effective. This would include many primary activities such as budgeting and individual managers' performance reviews. The idea here is to mainstream the new measures. Wherever potential conflicts or contradictions to the new set are found, they must be eliminated and replaced. Consistency of message and direction are critical.

As organizations begin to utilize the In-Sync measures, it will be found that the traditional budgeting philosophy is not congruent with the new system. The traditional top-down, line-item budgeting methodology is ill-suited to a synchronous environment. Although different companies have adopted a variety of different approaches in altering their systems, some common elements have emerged.

Primarily these have revolved around the concept of enhanced flexibility at the operating level. Accountability is not necessarily lost through this process in that budgets are based upon **maintaining** a predetermined T/OE ratio. The budget development process should be characterized as a "bottom up" activity, with the T/OE ratio determining spending. Utilizing such an approach allows much more flexibility in day-to-day decision making, yet always maintaining profitability.

Incorporating the new measures into individual performance reviews is one of the most powerful means of communicating the new message. Certainly the measures **must** find their expression in the individual manager's and supervisor's activities and decisions. As such, incorporating them into the performance review process is a natural extension. The linkage of T, I, OE, and customer-based measures to the individual's compensation and status is an essential element in the transformation of the business. People have to understand this linkage if it is to be meaningful.

Implicit in this entire discussion is the notion that new measures will drive new behaviors and decision making. Obviously this requires that the horizontal and vertical organization understands which behaviors and decisions will move the measures in the "right" direction. It is the central responsibility of the management team to provide the appropriate training and tools (the methods) for the organization to be successful in the context of the new measures. A primary theme in this book has been the importance of correctly aligning the company's measures, methods, and mindset to the dictates of the marketplace. Attempting to change one, exclusive of the others, is the primary reason many improvement efforts have fallen short of expectations. To be successful in transforming a business into a world-class competitor, senior management must embrace a holistic approach.

A central element in the development and implementation process discussed in this chapter must be the provision of the proper tools to drive the measures in the "right" direction. Once the measures have been changed and institutionalized, senior management must seek to provide the organization with the training and tools required to optimize the "new" environment. It is not enough to simply change the "scorecard" for the game, people must be trained and given the opportunity to embrace alternate methods which will yield the results required under the new approach. Don't expect that these tools will simply emerge because the rules have changed.

There exists a wide variety of management tools which can be selectively provided to the organization in the change process. It is a primary responsibility of senior management to determine which are the most appropriate for the task at hand. Further, it is critical that the variety of tools selected work in a complementary fashion. Each of the elements of the improvement effort should fit together into a coherent strategy.

References

1. Srikanth, Mokshagundam L. and Mike Umble. <u>Synchronous Manufacturing: Principles for World-Class Excellence</u>. Cincinnati: South-Western Publishing Co., 1990.

2. Cox, Jeff and Eliyahu M. Goldratt. <u>The Goal</u>. Great Barrington: North River Press, Inc., 1992.

3. Cavallaro, Harold E. A. Jr. and Mokshagundam L. Srikanth. <u>Regaining Competitiveness: Putting *The Goal* To Work</u>. New Haven: The Spectrum Publishing Company, 1990.

4. Johnson, Thomas H. and Robert S. Kaplan. <u>Relevance Lost: The Rise and Fall of Management Accounting</u>. Boston: Harvard Business School Press, 1987.

5. Kaplan, Robert S. and David P. Norton. "The Balanced Scorecard: Measures That Drive Performance." <u>Harvard Business Review</u> February 1992: 71-79.

6. Dertouzos, Michael L. and Richard K. Lester, Robert M. Solow, and the MIT Commission on Industrial Productivity. <u>Made In America: Regaining the Productive Edge.</u> Cambridge: The MIT Press, 1989.

About the authors

Dr. Mokshagundam (Shri) L. Srikanth is the Managing Principal of The Spectrum Management Group, Inc. Prior to founding Spectrum Management, he worked closely with Dr. Eli Goldratt as Senior Research Fellow and Director of Operations at Creative Output, Inc. Dr. Srikanth is the author of two books: 1) *Synchronous Manufacturing: Principles for World-Class Excellence* (with Professor Mike Umble), and 2) *Regaining Competitiveness: Putting 'The Goal' To Work* (with Harold Cavallaro). Dr. Srikanth received his doctorate in Physics from Boston University.

Mr. Scott A. Robertson is a Principal of The Spectrum Management Group, Inc. He has an extensive background in materials management in a variety of industries. Mr. Robertson's practice within Spectrum is focused on the Aerospace and Defense industries. Prior to joining Spectrum Management, he worked at Creative Output, Inc., with Dr. Goldratt. Mr. Robertson received his B.S. from Ohio Wesleyan University.

Both have spoken and written widely on the subject of synchronous management and issues arising from its implementation.

The Spectrum Management Group, Inc., works with manufacturing companies to help change the culture or mindset, the operational measures, the operating methods, and the management structures so as to align them with the competitive needs of the marketplace. Spectrum Management has enabled its client companies to improve delivery performance and reduce lead times, while decreasing investment in inventories and resources. Their experience in the implementation of synchronous management techniques covers a broad cross-section of industries including Aerospace and Defense, Automotive, Furniture, Textiles, Consumer, and Industrial Products.